TWAYNE'S WORLD AUTHORS SERIES
A Survey of the World's Literature

JAPAN

Roy B. Teele, University of Texas, Austin

EDITOR

Kaneko Mitsuharu

TWAS 555

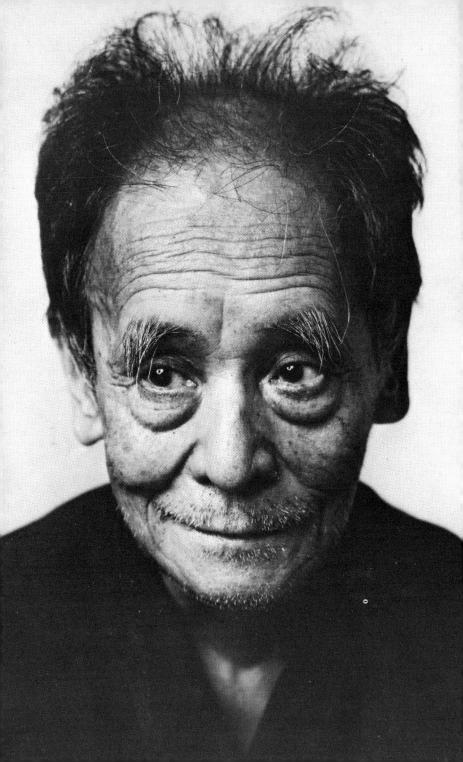

KANEKO MITSUHARU

By JAMES R. MORITA

The Ohio State University

TWAYNE PUBLISHERS

A DIVISION OF G. K. HALL & CO., BOSTON

Published in 1980 by Twayne Publishers,
A Division of G. K. Hall & Co.
All Rights Reserved

Printed on permanent/durable acid-free paper and bound
in the United States of America

First Printing

Photograph Courtesy of Mori Ken

Library of Congress Cataloging in Publication Data

Morita, James R
Kaneko Mitsuharu.

(Twayne's world authors series ; TWAS 555 : Japan)
Bibliography: p. 148–52
Includes index.
1. Kaneko, Mitsuharu, 1895-1975.
2. Authors, Japanese—20th century—Biography.
PL832.A6Z76   895.6′1′4   79-920
ISBN 0-8057-6397-X

Contents

About the Author

James R. Morita has published studies, translations and reviews, mostly of modern Japanese poetry, in both English and Japanese books and journals, which include *Contemporary Japanese Literature* (1977), *Miyazawa Kenji kenkyū sōsho* (1975), *Monumenta Nipponica, Literature East and West, International Poetry Review, Hon'yaku no sekai,* and *Journal of the Association of Teachers of Japanese.* He studied English at Okayama University, Japan, and lived in various cities in the United States. During the course of living, he earned Master's Degrees from the University of Michigan and, for eight years, he was Japanese Bibliographer at the Far Eastern Library of the University of Chicago. In 1968 he received a Ph.D. in Far Eastern Languages and Civilizations from the University of Chicago for his dissertation on a Japanese novelist. Dr. Morita has taught at the University of Chicago and the University of Oregon before he joined the faculty of the Ohio State University, where he is Associate Professor of East Asian Languages and Literatures.

Preface

As early as the eighth century, the Japanese had gathered together *man'yō*, or "ten thousand leaves," many poems by ordinary men as well as poets, to make up a great anthology. Known as *The Manyoshu*, the anthology contains excellent works on various subjects and in various forms, in language which has remained basically unchanged. Inasmuch as *The Manyoshu* has served for centuries as a constant source of inspiration for poets, as a major object of study for scholars, and as a perpetual source of nostalgia for people, the Japanese have been nurtured in such a way that they have been able to produce anthologies and collections, uniquely representing the temperament and mood of the succeeding periods. Japan has always been a country of poetry and the Japanese have always written poems as an integral part of their way of life.

Of course, poetic forms have changed somewhat, as have other elements in their poetry. In the modern period, European poetry was studied, translated, and imitated, so that Japanese poetry underwent changes not only in form, but also in style, subject matter, and theme. Innumerable poets appeared, forming groups or societies. Many of these groups organized, published journals, then disbanded, merged into others, or were reorganized under different names. Some were intrigued by Symbolism. Others were deeply impressed by Dadaism, finding therein an affinity to Zen. Many were professed Marxists or anarchists. Others adhered to lyricism. There was a group which advocated a short form of poetry almost like the seventeen-syllable *haiku*. One group supported T. S. Eliot's intellectual style and published generally long poems in their journal called *Arechi (The Wasteland)*. One group tried to implant the sonnet form. In addition, there was an even greater number of poets who specialized in the traditional thirty-one-syllable *tanka* or in the shorter *haiku*. Then there was an influential critic who attacked *haiku* as being a secondary art. If the Japanese were to compile another *Manyoshu*, they would have to comb through these poets, works, journals, anthologies, and individual collections; they might end up with literally 10,000 poets' works, still leaving out countless private publications. Privately published poetry collections are now so scattered that the majority of them may never be cataloged except by the authors and their circles. The point is that the enormous popularity of poetry has never diminished in Japan.

Just as a few poets were outstanding in each period, so there are such poets in the modern period who will probably remain preeminent in the future. Kaneko Mitsuharu is one of them. "The Self" was the object of Kaneko's lifelong search. Lack of the Self was the object of his pity and anger. Kaneko placed the masses of humanity under his critical gaze, and detested men lacking Self—the opportunist, the hypocrite, and the like. Few other writers were as keen as Kaneko in the study of man. No other poet wrote so much about the Japanese or himself.

Kaneko did not really belong to any literary circle, however. He rejected all ties, whether personal, political, or otherwise, and maintained his integrity. In one of his poems, "A Seal," he cautioned that the majority might not be always right, and wrote:

It was they who expelled Voltaire and imprisoned Grotius; those same creatures pollute the earth, from Batavia to Lisbon, with gossip and dust.

Those who sneeze and spit through their whiskers; those with prudish airs and stiffling yawns; those noisy groups pointing fingers at and accusing anyone who deviates from conventional standards, labeling him a traitor or madman. They intermarry to maintain this trait. They are of the same blood; they belong to the same clique. Their innumerable ties and the resulting wall of bodies block even the ocean current.

Anything untrue to itself, any injustice or insubstantiality, also fell into Kaneko's category of "detestable." He gave expression to his revulsion by singing of the true, the just, and the genuine. And he was persistent in doing so. Between the 1910s and his death in 1975, Kaneko published nearly twenty

volumes of poetry and about an equal number of collections of
essays, as well as several translations of Western works.

However, he seldom revealed his own Self. Usually he hid
it under his beguiling imagery built up of brilliantly chosen
language. The layers of imagery in his poetry are like Salvador
Dali's paintings: they offer different interpretations depend-
ing on how the reader perceives them. The seal, the animal at
sea, for example, could be a symbol of a domineering col-
onialist, or even a naval weapon, while at the same time it was
the meandering poet himself. In other words, he was a master
technician, too. Kaneko possessed a magic hand like other fine
poets who, while observing the outside world, immersed
themselves deeply in the inner world of the soul.

Yet, he was aware of his inescapable plight, being himself
one of the "seals" he hated. At such times, he sublimated his
pity and anger to understanding and love. He was very human: he was the poet of pride and sorrow. The conclusion of
"A Seal" is:

Among the crowd, worshipping unanimously, casting long shadows,
Is one
Who disdainfully faces the other way.
It is I.
I, who hate seals,
Yet, after all, I am only a seal.
But,
"A seal who faces the other way."

Critics divide Kaneko's career into several distinct periods,
linking them to historic phases of Japan: emergence as an imperial nation, war years, and defeat in the Pacific. They claim
that his poetry flowed in reciprocal proportion to those phases,
and label him as a "poet of resistance." Some assign a great
significance to Kaneko's roaming through Southeast Asia and
Europe. They argue that he was indifferent to worldly events
and see his traveling as evidence of his nihilism. Others con-
jecture that he was influenced by a philosopher in the West
and see his wandering as a result of his nihilism. Those who
value antiwar poems take Kaneko's poems that sang about his
granddaughter as signs of degeneration. Moralists denounce
some of Kaneko's later works as indecent. The wide swing of
his poetic pendulum may indeed confuse the reader, but at the
same time it challenges him endlessly.

This book does not attempt to place Kaneko in any so-called established school or group. The author wishes to present to the West how a Japanese poet lived in modern times, what poems he wrote, and how he died. The periodization, which is reflected in the chapter divisions of the book, is made in a way the author considers appropriate to trace Kaneko's career. This periodization may suggest certain developmental stages of modern Japanese poetry. The book will incidentally disclose some literary episodes related to Japanese writers already known in the West, namely, Shimazaki Tōson, Kunikida Doppo, Yone Noguchi, Tanizaki Jun'ichirō, Yokomitsu Riichi, and Kusano Shimpei. It will also refer to numerous poets and poetry journals in order to show aspects of the history of modern Japanese poetry, which have yet to become known in the West. The translations, made contrary to the standard procedure ("from a foreign language to the native tongue"), are added in the hope of enhancing the above objectives. Only when the translations are complete and not excerpts are they preceded by the titles.

Throughout the book Japanese names will appear in Japanese order—the family name first and the given name second—at the first occurrence. Thereafter, for the sake of uniformity, family names alone will be employed. Even though a person is commonly remembered by his *gagō*, or "elegant pen name," in Japan, as in the case of Tōson, his family name, Shimazaki, is used in this book. Exceptions are Michiyo for Kaneko's wife, Mori Michiyo; Ken for his son, Mori Ken; Sōtarō for his foster father, Kaneko Sōtarō; Sumi for his foster mother, Kaneko Sumi; and a few others. Another exception is the popular family name Satō: five different writers named Satō, distinguished by their first names, will appear in the following pages. The dates of birth and death are indicated in parentheses where convenient. All titles of the Japanese works are translated. However, when they first appear, the originals are indicated in parentheses, e.g., "A Seal" (*"Ottosei"*) and *The Sharks* (*Samé*). Both the translated and original titles will be found in the Index at the end of the book.

Acknowledgments

The Japan Foundation's Professional Fellowship enabled me to complete this book in Japan during the latter half of 1977. I benefited greatly from the instruction, both direct and indirect, of Japanese scholars, critics, and poets. Mr. Hara Shirō, poet and fine lecturer of Waseda University, in particular, inspired me with his deep philosophy of literature; the critic and poet Nakajima Kaichirō helped me to straighten up chronological details; and Professor Shutō Motozumi of Kumamoto University taught me bibliographic and textual details. The staffs of Kindai Bungakkan, Waseda University Library, and the National Diet Library assisted me in locating materials and finding facts. The son of Kaneko Mitsuharu and Mori Michiyo, Professor Mori Ken, extended his encouragement to study and consent to translate Kaneko's poems. Professor Takeda Katsuhiko of Waseda expended precious time to facilitate my work. Dr. Taniguchi Sumio, my teacher, now of the Ministry of Education, was most considerate to make my stay in Japan rewarding.

It was Professor Roy E. Teele, editor of this series, who first conceived the idea of this book and, years ago, gave me the opportunity to write it. He thoroughly read and criticized my manuscript. He also permitted me to reprint in this book my translations published earlier in *Literature East and West*, which he edits. Colleen Scofield and Jon LaCure participated in the translation of a few poems at the University of Oregon in 1970. Thomas Cogan, a graduate student at the University of Hawaii, and Professor Keiko McDonald of the University of Pittsburgh acquired some rare journals and books for me in Tokyo in 1975 and 1976, respectively. My wife, Ichiko, carefully read manuscripts and offered many useful suggestions.

Professors Edwin McClellan of Yale, Howard S. Hibbett of Harvard, and William F. Sibley of the University of Chicago warmly supported my undertaking throughout.

The College of Humanities of The Ohio State University gave me a grant which made it possible for me to buy a *Kaneko Mitsuharu zenshū* and visit the libraries of the University of Chicago and the University of Michigan in summer of 1976. Professor Miles K. McElrath, chairman of the Department of East Asian Languages and Literatures, The Ohio State University, generously made arrangements with the College so that I could use my Faculty Development Quarter to free me from teaching duty in fall 1977. It was, however, Kaneko Mitsuharu's works themselves that sustained me most while I toiled.

JAMES R. MORITA

The Ohio State University

Chronology

1895 Ōshika Yasukazu born on December 25 near Nagoya.
1897 Adopted by the Kaneko family in Nagoya.
1901 Moves to Kyoto.
1906 Moves to Tokyo.
1907 Enters a French mission school.
1914 Enters Waseda University.
1915 Withdraws from Waseda University. Enters Ueno Art Academy, and quits in a few months. Enters Keio University and quits.
1919 Publishes *The House of Earthen Walls*. Travels to Europe.
1920 Stays in Brussels. Visits Paris.
1921 Returns to Japan. ·
1922 Edits *Paradise*.
1923 Publishes *A May Beetle*.
1924 Marries Mori Michiyo.
1925 Leaves Tokyo for Nagasaki and travels to Shanghai.
1926 Publishes *The Faltering*.
1927 Travels to Shanghai for the second time.
1928 Leaves Japan with Michiyo for China and Southeast Asia; arrives in Paris in 1930.
1931 Lives alone in Brussels.
1932 Returns to Japan via Singapore and lives in Tokyo.
1937 Publishes *The Sharks*. Travels to Peking.
1940 Publishes *The Journey through Malay and Dutch-India*.
1943 Vacates Tokyo to a village near Mount Fuji.
1946 Returns to Tokyo.
1948 Publishes *My Parachute* and *The Moth*.
1949 *An Elegy for Women* and *The Song of the Devil's Son*.
1952 *The Tragedy of Man*.
1955 *Inhumanity*.

1957 *The Poet.*

1959 *About the Japanese* and *About Japanese Art.*

1960 The first volume of the complete works.

1962 *The Song like a Fart.*

1965 *The IL* and *The History of Despair.*

1967 *The Tragedy of the Japanese, The Poems for Wakaba,* and *The Complete Poems by Kaneko Mitsuharu.*

1968 *Cruelty and Inhumanity* and *Love 69.*

1969 *Short Literary Essays by Kaneko Mitsuharu.* Suffers from a stroke.

1971 *A Skull, New Miscellaneous Notes, A Biography of the Inhuman, A Record of Transfiguration,* and a revised version of *The Poet.*

1973 *Sleep, Paris, The Perverse,* and *The Flower and an Empty Bottle.*

1974 *People, Please Be Generous* and *The West and the East.* Suffers from the second stroke. Works for two journals, *Half Serious* and *Just a Moment.*

1975 Dies on June 30.

CHAPTER 1

The House of Earthen Walls:
1895-1923

KANEKO Mitsuharu was born Ōshika Yasukazu on
December 25, 1895, in the countryside of Aichi, a prefecture in the center of Japan, now known for the large industrial
city of Nagoya. He was adopted by the Kaneko family in
Nagoya before he became two years old. Until 1919, when he
published his first collection of poems, *The House of Earthen
Walls* (*Akatsuchi no ie*), Kaneko used his real name, Kaneko
Yasukazu. He happened to notice, when he was twenty, that
his first name, Yasukazu, was registered in the official record
in characters different from those he had been using.[1] This is
perhaps comparable to someone's discovery that he had mis-
spelled his own first name for twenty years without realizing
the error. Mitsuharu was a pen name which he began using in
1923 when he published his second book of verse, *A May
Beetle* (*Koganemushi*).

Kaneko's real parents were not educated people. His father
did not have a steady job. At one time he was a local agent for
traveling entertainers; at another he was a speculator in real
estate. His mother was the type of woman who was completely
submissive to her husband, working hard all the time to raise
the family. She once tried to continue an old family trade of
selling *saké*, but failed. In 1896 Kaneko's parents moved out of
their native province and came to Nagoya. Kaneko had two
older brothers. His younger sister and brother had not yet
been born.

In Nagoya his father continued to be jobless, associating
with such people as political bullies and gamblers. He was
never successful in land speculation. His mother, when she
was very busy, would leave Kaneko with a distant relative who
owned a small hairdressing shop. Kaneko was not shy of stran-

15

gers, and soon he was a pet of the shop's customers. One cus-
tomer, the sixteen-year-old wife of a wealthy man, saw Kaneko
playing in a corner of the shop and picked him up. She did not
put him down before she had made up her mind to adopt him.
This young wife was Kaneko Sumi, a daughter of one of the
directors of the prosperous Tokyo construction firm called
Shimizu & Co. Sumi asked her husband, Kaneko Sōtarō, then
the head of the Nagoya office of Shimizu & Co., to negotiate
the adoption with the Ōshika. Kaneko's parents were in no
condition to decline Sōtarō's offer, and in 1897 Ōshika
Yasukazu became Kaneko Yasukazu. Kaneko did not particularly miss his real parents. For Sumi the arrangement was like
buying a doll: she did and undid, in as many different styles as
her moods, the hair of her adopted son.

Japan in the 1890s retained much of its traditional values
and customs. Nagoya took pride in being the home of the To-
kugawa, the powerful clan that ruled Japan immediately pre-
ceding the modern period. In the Kaneko family, however,
there was a dichotomy of the old and the new. Along with the
old social mores and conventions there was something new,
Sōtarō and Sumi's liking for the fashionable, as represented by
imported canned soup and cookies which were lavishly consumed in the household. On the one hand, the family observed festivals and seasonal routines in the same superstiti-
ous manner as their ancestors had done. On the other, Sōtarō
threw Western-style parties for carpenters and bricklayers as
well as for architects and bankers at his large house. He also
frequently entertained his business friends in restaurants and
the licensed quarters. On many of these occasions Kaneko was
the pet of the guests, dancers, musicians, and jesters.

In the back of the house there was a family warehouse
which was, for protection from fire and burglary, made of
earth. This earthen-walled warehouse offered Kaneko a quiet
hiding place among the piles of dining wares, picture scrolls,
calligraphy scrolls, sutras, children's books and Chinese and
Japanese classics, as well as many rare imported artifacts. The
atmosphere of the warehouse never failed to facinate Kaneko.
Sometimes, antique dealers and import-export traders walked
in and broke Kaneko's daydreams. They sold dubious objects
to Sōtarō and often took some things out of the warehouse. The
whole house somehow smelled of immorality and decay.

Two sisters of Sōtarō also lived in the house. Sumi would chat and eat with them, while Sōtarō was at work. Often they played a phonograph, a rare, expensive commodity affordable only by rich families at the time. They also read story books aloud, looked at old, mysterious picture books, and giggled. Occasionally they dressed Kaneko like a girl and strolled in downtown Nagoya together. Motion pictures were not yet available, but there were shadow plays which aroused fantasies and excitement in the minds of women and children. At night the women took turns hugging Kaneko in their bed. The young Kaneko could not forget the peculiar movements of the shadows for a long time.

Japan had just won a major war against China and the possession of Taiwan and its adjacent islands. As a result, the Japanese were elated, and the nation's economy was booming. Construction firms were particularly busy. Shimizu & Co. concluded a large contract with the government to build forts in the new territory. Sōtarō was sent to Taiwan to oversee the work, and rarely spent time with his family in those days. Kaneko, often hiding himself in the earthen-walled warehouse, continued to be the center of attention in the family. When Sōtarō returned to Japan, he was promoted to director of the company's Kyoto office. Kaneko moved to Kyoto in 1901.

Kyoto was an old city where the emperor had resided until the 1860s. It was already Japan's capital at the end of the eighth century, and for a long time it was the cultural as well as political center of the country. When Kaneko moved there, the customs and manners in Kyoto seemed more strictly bound by tradition than in Nagoya. Most people still wore the rather unfunctional kimono, and they spoke slowly and with an accent. Kaneko, who had tasted an unusual mixture of attention and negligence and of joy and loneliness at heart, sensed the tradition stagnating and the people suffocating under the low roof tiles of the old houses in Kyoto. The area around the old imperial palace was quiet, and many temples and shrines were on the decline. There were no modern industries of note; only small-scale crafts supported the city's economy. Kaneko noticed many families in his neighborhood making a living by selling their daughters into the licensed quarters or both husband and wife doing some miscellaneous work for houses of prostitution. He would hear surprisingly obscene conversations carried on routinely. One day he saw young children of his age engaging in a certain act in the back of a lumberyard near his house. Though shocking, the act was not entirely unfamiliar to Kaneko: he had seen it in the old picture books in the warehouse. In no time Kaneko was a member of the *enfants terribles*. At first, however, he felt his knees trembling and he could hardly hold himself up. Soon he found himself hurrying to the hideout as soon as he got off school, filled with excitement, expectation, and a certain sense of guilt.

In 1904 Japan was victorious in another major war, this time against powerful Russia. Disturbing the stillness of Kyoto, the bells of newspaper boys announcing extras sounded on the streets every day. There were celebrations. The people, both old and young, paraded through the streets, changing the atmosphere of the quiet city of Kyoto. Kaneko liked gaiety; he enjoyed the noise, the excitement, and the arousal of his desires. Sōtarō's business prospered, and he rarely stayed home because of many business meetings. In 1906 he was transferred to the main office in Tokyo and the family had to move again. Kaneko bid farewell to the lumberyard and, unable to say a word to a girl of whom he was very fond, left Kyoto.

Tokyo was flourishing as the new capital of Japan, which had become an indisputable major power in the world. Adjustment to the new life was difficult for the nine-year-old, sensitive boy. For one thing, both Sōtarō and Sumi, involved in their own adjustments, spent less time with Kaneko. And the pace of life was quicker; things were newer, and the people seemed more liberated. At least there were more people wearing Western clothes. The influence of Western culture was indeed more apparent in everything and the whole atmosphere was much different from that of Kyoto. Department stores were rising and the imported merchandise in them was fascinating. What bothered Kaneko most, however, was the language:his slow Kyoto accent was laughed at by his classmates. He tried to master Tokyo speech, but his attempts at quick imitation were considered too unnatural, and some classmates treated Kaneko cruelly. He felt he needed somehow to gain the favor of his classmates and regain his confidence and pride. Before he knew it, Kaneko was a habitual shoplifter in the neighborhood stores. Furthermore, he was soon heading a small gang of shoplifters, until one day he was caught by a store guard. Neither Sōtarō nor Sumi, of course, had noticed Kaneko's habit. It had been some time since his family paid much attention to the adopted son. Nevertheless, he was confined in the family warehouse as punishment for as long as fifteen days. He did not admit his guilt to his foster parents, fearing that, if he did, his *raison d'être* might be lost.

The family moved to another part of Tokyo, and Kaneko had to change schools again. His licentiousness did not change in the new school. He was rebellious against his foster parents, his having to move around, and his fate. One day he and his friend visited a Yoshiwara geisha, whom he knew Sōtarō was patronizing. Politely refused service, the boys felt very much insulted, and they immediately decided to seek freedom in America. The next morning Kaneko, the friend, and one other boy left their houses with the full intention of getting out of Japan. They hitchhiked on a horse cart to Yokohama, the large seaport southwest of Tokyo, in order to stow away on a ship. While staying with the friend's relative in Yokohama, however, all but Kaneko lost the heart to escape, and they decided to go back home. They managed to return to Tokyo, sleeping outdoors. The parents had notified the police that the boys were missing, and when Kaneko was sitting alone on the steps of a Shinto shrine, unable to walk farther, he was discovered by a family acquaintance.

The year 1906 was noteworthy in the history of Japanese literature. In that year Shimazaki Tōson (1872-1943), who had been regarded as the most important poet, published his first long novel, *The Broken Commandment (Hakai)*. This event signified two things: it ended the period of *shintaishi*, or the new-style poetry, which Shimazaki himself was most instrumental in creating, and it heralded the coming of naturalist novels into the world of Japanese prose fiction.

Shintaishi, which had flourished before that time, was in fact a quite successful marriage of traditional Japanese poetry and Western poetry. Inspired especially by English romantic poems, Japanese poetry had undergone considerable changes in only a few decades at the end of the nineteenth century. Unlike the seventeen-syllable *haiku* or the thirty-one syllable *tanka*, *shintaishi* was longer and, like Western poetry, it was divided into stanzas. However, it still adhered to the traditional prosodic technique of combining five and seven syllables. Some *shintaishi* tried to break further away from the traditional poetry in terms of both technique and content, but many retained the same subtle emotions that the Japanese had expressed a long time ago through the images of autumn wind, snow, flowers, flowing water, and the like. One of the difficulties of *shintaishi*, then, was that it was restricted from its outset by both the form and the treatment of the subject matter. Therefore, although it brought a fresh breeze into the world of Japanese letters, exciting many young readers, it was less attractive to the serious reader whose intellect and emotions grew quickly.

Shimazaki's *The Broken Commandment* was a response to the demands posed by both the public and himself for literature matching the complexity of the times. It was the story of a schoolteacher who had been commanded by his father never to reveal the fact that he was of the parish *eta* class. The young teacher could not help showing publicly his sympathy for an *eta* boy, an *eta* politician, and others of the same suppressed social class, and, after much mental anguish, he made a public confession of his identity. The poet-turned-novelist, Shimazaki, ended this novel with a scene in which the hero decided to go to Texas. This ending, later criticized by some as a novelistic shortcoming, may really have been appropriate for a naturalist novel. The "romantic" age of *shintaishi* was passing and the age of "realism" was coming. Dissatisfied ex-samurai, frustrated farmers, ambitious businessmen, young men of foresight, and rebellious men like Kaneko all wished to go to the New World in those days. To learn from the West in order to become as "civilized" and materially rich as Europeans and Americans was the attitude common to many Japanese at that time.

In April 1907 Kaneko chose to enter a French mission school named Gyōsei Junior High School. He had been attracted by the school's uniform which, with shiny golden buttons, seemed to symbolize the glory of the Western civilization. Besides, he knew that the prestigious public schools were too high in academic standards for him to be accepted. Thus, he started to learn French. It did not take much time, however, for Kaneko to discover that the school was very strict and study was difficult. He disliked the school's regimentation and system of cramming for exams. At year's end he received bad grades for most subjects except art and Chinese literature. He could understand the good grade in art, for he had studied drawing with a tutor before and he knew he excelled in it. As for Chinese literature, it was the teacher rather than literature that attracted him. Kaneko was fond of the teacher who, though nicknamed "Fake Sage," was a righteous man. Like an ancient Chinese scholar, Fake Sage would criticize the political decay, attack moral degeneration, and lament his hard lot in life. Charmed particularly by his outspokenness, Kaneko saw the truth in his remarks. To him, Fake Sage, who was apparently not well paid, was a far better teacher than others and a more reliable man than his foster father. Besides, he found the Chinese literature text more interesting than the French grammar book, so when he finished the textbook he proceeded to read Chinese classics, historical documents, and novels. Sōtarō's warehouse came in handy, providing him with more books and the privacy in which to read.

This interest gave him a good excuse for not attending school. He stayed home, occasionally visited antiquarian bookstores, and quickly expanded the scope of his reading from Chinese to Japanese literature. He was particularly attracted by the early nineteenth-century Japanese "light", or popular, erotic novels, which were banal but peculiarly realistic in depiction. Then Kaneko came to admire the dilettante authors of the "light" novels, who detested power and injustice and, though dissipating in the licensed quarter, attained a high level of understanding of art and life. He sympathized with the repressed talents, those whose efforts and desires were crushed under the unjust system. He learned that those who were politically powerful and socially successful were not always righteous or noble.

By the end of his sophomore year Kaneko knew that he had read more Japanese literature than any of his classmates. Yet he felt uneasy. He could not convince himself that his deepening interest in and understanding of literature were of any value, and wondered if only material things were worthwhile in life. Advancement to his junior year was at stake and he needed a higher grade. He wanted to have strength—physical excellence might give him confidence. Those were days of

youthful agony and blind search: as he struggled, he went
deeper into perfecting his dissipation. It was not difficult to
find companions in his endeavor. It was not difficult, either, to
obtain money from Sōtarō or Sumi. On school days Kaneko got
together with a few comrades, and they changed their school
uniforms to fashionable clothes and strolled downtown, in
parks, theaters, amusement parlors, and licensed quarters. As
a result, he failed to move up to the next grade. He tried to
transfer to another school, but did not pass the transfer exam-
ination.

A year after Shimazaki published *The Broken Commandment*, Tayama Katai (1871-1930), who had also written some
shintaishi, published a novel called *The Quilt (Futon)*. The
literary world had not yet recovered from the shock and excitement caused by *The Broken Commandment*. Now *The
Quilt*, apparently based on the author's private life, immediately became a subject of controversy. Some praised
Tayama's honesty expressed in the novel, while some denounced the work's moral implications. One critic noted that
with *The Quilt* the naturalist novel was firmly established in
Japan. *The Quilt* depicted, in unadorned language, a love affair between a married novelist and a young woman who
studied literature under him. At the story's end, the
novelist—presumably Tayama—wept into the filthy quilt
which the young woman had left behind. Kaneko and his
friends talked about *The Quilt* and continued to discuss such
favorite topics as love, life, and death. They indulged in an
endless discussion on the problem of Platonic love versus
physical love; they talked about Beatrice the eternal woman.
The times were such that the eternal woman tended to be de-
graded. Platonic love was not held in high esteem, at least in
Kaneko's circle.

One of those days in 1910, Kaneko skipped school and went
to an archery club. With his money and time, he had been a
good member of the club. That day he met a man called
Nakane Komajūrō. Looking older and better educated than
Kaneko, Nakane was not a delinquent student; he was a managing editor of the famous publisher Shinchōsha. Kaneko did
not miss the chance: he asked Nakane what the greatest contemporary Japanese novel was. Nakane's answer was short,

but decisive. He said, "Tokuda Shūsei's [1871-1943] *The Mould* [*Kabi*]."

Kaneko read Tokuda's *The Mould*. He found that it was similar to Tayama's *The Quilt* in subject matter and treatment, and thought that he obtained a better idea of what naturalist literature was like. He considered that Tokuda's drawn-out description possessed neither grace nor intensity, but his penetrating approach to the subject matter was impressive. Furthermore, he felt a great empathy with the author, who depicted, without either Shimazaki's humanitarian interpretation or Tayama's sentimentalism, the agony of a character falling in love with his housemaid's daughter. There was an immediate resemblance between Kaneko's aimless life and the hero's: he had developed a relationship with a housemaid named Haru at that time. Within the same year he tried his hand at a no-longer-extant novel, known only as *Hokorobi*. Perhaps he needed catharsis, and looked at literature as such. At any rate, Kaneko was definitely becoming inclined toward literature.

In those years, the Japanese Literature Department of Waseda University in Tokyo was attracting many students who aspired to be novelists. Contrary to a few decades before, it was no longer considered debased for educated men to become novelists. In the English Department there was Tsubouchi Shōyō (1859-1935), who wrote Japan's first important theory of the novel along with some experimental novels in the 1880s.

Tsubouchi and other Waseda people were editing the influential journal *Waseda Literature* (*Waseda bungaku*), which reviewed many important current novels and published original works. Overall, Waseda University was regarded by many as a stronghold of the Naturalist literary movement. Kaneko, feeling empathy with the world of Tayama and Tokuda, thought that Waseda might guide him to some meaningful direction. In April 1914 he gained admission to Waseda. However, preoccupied with activities outside of school, he did not attend many classes. Lectures on literature did not seem to him the same as literature itself, and literature did not seem to him equal to the excitement, sorrow, and joy in life. By then his dilettantism was so advanced that his ideal was to live a life of both Dorian Gray and the nihilist lover Sanin at the same time. He was attracted more by the lives of the characters than by those of Oscar Wilde and Mikhail P. Artsybashev. The most significant goal in life seemed to him to enjoy life to his heart's content and to die at the peak of his youth. Leading a dissipated life, he could not rid himself of the idea that literature is a mere accessory to real life.

Kaneko withdrew from Waseda University in the beginning of 1915, and then entered the Japanese Painting Department of the Ueno Art Academy, only to quit it in three months. In September of that year, he was enrolled in another private school in Tokyo, this time, Keiō University. However, because of the First World War, Kaneko had to take the induction physical. He was not drafted, but instead he was given a warning by the physician of his poor state of health. At the age of nineteen, he weighed less than ninety pounds. It was evident that not only his heart was in bad condition, but his body had also deteriorated badly. He noticed that he was not sleeping well, suffering from nightmares and perspiring in bed. Confused and fearing death, Kaneko continued to lead a fast life. He drank *saké*, too. His friends, who were not many to begin with, left him, and the few who remained friendly doubted his sanity. As for Kaneko's foster parents, Sōtarō was not particularly opposed to Kaneko's dissipation per se, only warning him about venereal disease. Sumi, still childless and unhappy with Sōtarō, did not care for her debauched adopted son. Kaneko was irritated with the family, the friends, the women, and himself, finding any plan for the future or any regular schedule very bothersome.

Kaneko was diagnosed as having capillary bronchitis and ordered to stay in bed. Among the people who inquired after Kaneko were Hoizumi Yoshisuke and Hoizumi Yoshichika, brothers, who were members of a small "literary" club. The club had its headquarters in the licensed quarter, Yoshiwara, and the members wore stylish clogs resembling the high-heeled sandals of the Yoshiwara geisha. The elder Hoizumi was an argumentative critic of all things, whereas his brother was a lyricist. It was Hoizumi, the younger, who drew Kaneko into writing poems. One of Kaneko's poems from this period is reported to be:

Opposition

When I was a boy
I was opposed to school.
I am still opposed
To working to make a living.

I dislike first of all
Health, justice, and such.
Man loses his senses
If healthy and just.

Of course I am opposed
To patriotism or humanity.
I am opposed to government
The world of writers and artists.

If asked what I was born for
My answer is: "To oppose."
I in the east
Longing for the west.

Clothes reversed, shoes on the wrong feet
Pants twisted, I mount a horse backward.
What others hate is my favorite.
To be displeased is my pleasure.

To oppose is to live,
A noble act, I think.
Opposition is life
The way to find my Self.[2]

When Kaneko recovered from bronchitis, he did not return
to Keiō University. A new interest had captured him, and he
continued to read poetry. Among the works he read were
**European poems translated into Japanese by Mori Ōgai
(1862-1922), Ueda Bin (1874-1916), and Nagai Kafū (1876-
1959).** It was indeed fortunate for Kaneko and, for that matter,
for modern Japanese poetry that these translators were both
scholarly and artistic. Through reading German Romantic,
French Parnassian, and Symbolist poets in these excellent
translations, Kaneko learned of poetry different from

Hoizumi's. He also realized that the Naturalist realism he had thought he was practicing in life was quite obsolete in the world of letters. When he turned his eye to contemporary Japanese poetry, he noticed that it was dominated by two poets, Kitahara Hakushū (1885-1942) and Miki Rofū (1889-1964), and that both were enjoying their reputation as "Symbolists." It appeared that the period of *shintaishi* was completely in the past, and many poets were using the colloquial language in a freer manner than before. New poets unanimously ignored the old prosodic technique of combining five and seven syllables. Kaneko read works by such poets as Hitomi Tōmei (1883-1974) and Yamamura Bochō (1884-1924), in addition to those by Kitahara and Miki. In all, he found new poems possessing something definitely appealing to his sensitivity. He wrote more poems and showed them to Hoizumi. Just at that time he was informed of Sōtarō's terminal illness.

The impending death of Sōtarō did not bother Kaneko. He would go to Sōtarō's bedroom and, as he was asked, spread out the family treasures, paintings and calligraphy from the warehouse, and joined him in appreciating them. He doubted that many items, for which he knew Sōtarō had spent a fortune, were genuine, but of course he did not tell that to Sōtarō. There was another thing he did not wish to tell the dying man. He had determined not to tell Sōtarō what he had witnessed with his own eyes: Sumi's affair with a neighbor. Conjugal relations between Sōtarō and Sumi had long ago deteriorated. And Kaneko himself continued to lead a debauched life, having relations with a cousin who came to see Sōtarō and with Sōtarō's nurse. In October 1916 Sōtarō died of stomach cancer.

Knowing all about greed as well as lust, Kaneko fought off many relatives who appeared in the hope of inheriting part of Sōtarō's estate. Some relatives openly attacked Kaneko for his dissipated life and argued against Kaneko's inheriting anything at all from Sōtarō, but Kaneko did not submit to any pressure and split the legacy with Sumi. The total inheritance came to about 200,000 yen each, which was considerable at that time, when most people's salary was well below 100 yen a month. However, Sumi spent hers to support her lover, and Kaneko used his for causes he did not even care much about. His real father appeared and took some money. His real brother showed up, too. Kaneko grew listless, tired, and sick. He later wrote about this time:

Something went wrong at the outset, and I was helpless victim of circumstances—I have not been able to rid myself of this way of thinking since I turned twenty. . . . This sense of failure has stayed with me as an inferiority complex. I have not accomplished anything: I am dissatisfied. I am listless, and I cannot exert my strength at important moments in life. Even at the time I could have redeemed my failure in the past, I have let the chance pass by not doing what I really should have done.

I did not intend to be either a poet or an artist. I did not want to be a politican, a general, a merchant, or an adventurer, either. I only wished that I had been blessed with exquisite beauty, so I could die before the beauty faded. If only that had been possible, I would not have wanted even love.[3]

Early in 1917 Kaneko was diagnosed as having tuberculosis and was hospitalized. It was a timely break. As he rested alone in the hospital, he tried to get back to his recent love—poetry. He wrote poems and kept them in his notebook. When he was discharged from the hospital, he found that Sumi had moved out of the house to live with her lover. Sumi and Kaneko sold the house, and Kaneko too moved to a rented house. Unable to settle down, he traveled to many places, ostensibly to regain his health but really to search for his soul. Shortly he moved again to another rented house in Tokyo and started to entertain his friends who had resumed their friendship with him. Kaneko had his own money now. Toward the end of 1917 he and his friends launched a literary magazine which they named *The House of Souls (Tamashii no ie)*. He financed it, but the magazine was published only three times before the members lost interest in it.

In 1918 Kaneko invested his money heavily in a manganese mine not far from Tokyo, following the suggestion of his real father, who had recently come back into his life. Kaneko wore a stylish hunting suit, carried a hammer at his waist, walked in the mountains, and at night threw parties for engineers, realtors, landowners, and local geishas. Because of the First World War, manganese was in great demand, and mining in Japan was booming. In about a month, however, Kaneko discovered that merchants were incurably greedy, business was hypocritical, and mine investment was not necessarily profitable.

As soon as he returned to Tokyo, Kaneko visited the poet Kawaji Ryūkō (1888-1959) and asked him to find a reliable publisher for his poems. Kaneko had never met Kawaji, but he

had found Kawaji's poems, written in an entirely new free
style, more appealing to him than any other contemporary
poems. To him, Kawaji's poems on dirty subjects, such as
trash, were more "symbolic" than those by others who favored
a periphrastic depiction of only the elegant. Besides, Kawaji
reminded Kaneko of Walt Whitman, whose translated poems
he had read with great interest. It was unfair, Kaneko felt, that
Kawaji was overshadowed by the popularity of Kitahara and
Miki. As far as he had read, he had not found any other
Japanese poet heading in the direction which he thought
poetry should be developing. The times were such that democracy was discussed along with socialism among Japanese
intellectuals, and Whitman had an impact on younger writers
who were looking for a replacement for Symbolism. As
Kaneko introduced himself to Kawaji, Kawaji asked him if he
was a university student. Kaneko immediately answered that
he was "a humbug," which in Japanese was a pun on "a mine
speculator."

Kaneko's first collection of poems, *The House of Earthen
Walls* (*Akatsuchi no ie*), was published in 1919 by a small publisher with Kawaji's aid. Kaneko "invested" 500 yen to print it,
and the book was beautifully finished and hardbound. The
friends who had worked for the now defunct *The House of
Souls* were envious, but they congratulated Kaneko on his
venture. Critics, however, completely ignored *The House of
Earthen Walls*: the book sold less than ten copies.[4] Later,
Kaneko himself tended not to recognize this as his first book.

The House of Earthen Walls included a tender poem entitled "A Little Snake" ("*Kohebi*"), in which the poet compared
himself to a snake. He wrote that he was born slim like a
snake; he was pale; he was unable to stand, and he slithered
on a cursed road. The poem continued:

> But my friend
> My love
> O everyone
> Care for me no more
> I too will stop protecting myself
> Rather build a fence
> To limit my movements
>
> For I've freed myself from the bond called "man"
> To absorb the sun on my back

> So I'll give you
> Those things you cherish
> For I was reborn as a sly little snake[5]

Here is the birth of a poet who, like a little snake, is basically a
shy, self-conscious loner. He is ugly, detested, and sinful, but
he is free and independent, and he shines reflecting the sun.
In him are found symbolism, a flash of cynicism, the poet's
basic attitude toward man and society, and his understanding
of poetry as an instrument of the search for the soul.

The House of Earthen Walls contains nineteen other poems
revealing the young Kaneko. The one called "To 'The House
of Earthen Walls' " (" '*Akatsuchi no ie' ni*") may be noted for
its title and content. It depicts the poet in the earthen-walled
warehouse of his old house, and apparently indicates the main
theme of the book. The poet's youthful skepticism and intros-
pection are evident. And clearly, he has moved out of the dim,
secret world of self-indulgence. The poem reads, in part:

> How can a small circle
> A little chain of thoughts
> Be of use in the future?
> Look
> At the earthen color
> More antiquated than any
>
> Oh the secret in the attic
> Crumbling reasons and logic
> Aren't you foolish
> To consume your life in it?[6]

After some more exchange of rhetorical questions with the
second-person "you," who is the poet's other self, the poem is
concluded in the following stanza. The poet regrets having
wasted his youth in the warehouse attic.

> The door at which there is no one
> Chasing a mirage, my ideal
> I knock it till my fists bleed
>
> Soon time passes, years go by
> And women, with cold eyes, pretend to entice me
> I blame myself for this irreversible life
>
> "Why did I not look for it at another place?"[7]

It was at this opportune time that an old man by the name of Suzuki Kōjirō came to see Kaneko. Kaneko remembered him. A friend of Sōtarō, Suzuki was an antique dealer who had been to Europe on business several times and had occasionally entered the Kaneko family warehouse. Without a second thought, Kaneko accepted the old man's proposition to go to Europe with him and deposited a sum of 3,000 yen with Suzuki. The excitement of going abroad made Kaneko forget the displeasure of his discovery that this deposit also covered Suzuki's travel expenses. Kaneko had a formal suit tailored and bought a silk hat. A handful of friends, who included Fukushi Kōjirō (1889-1946), then a critic of "Symbolist" poets, gave him a party to celebrate both the publication of his first book and his first trip abroad.

Accompanied by Suzuki, Kaneko left Japan in December 1919 on the S.S. *Sado*, an old Japanese boat sailing to Europe for the first time since the end of the First World War. A victorious mood had overtaken the ship, and the passengers, Japanese and European alike, were excited. In a large third-class cabin some sang military marches aloud, some drank *saké*, some played cards, and some offered prayers. Many Japanese passengers were laborers for the Japanese establishments in Southeast Asia, such as rubber plantations, newspaper companies, and trading firms. There was a group of women whom Kaneko knew to be prostitutes going south to earn money in order to support their parents. At night the Japanese passengers gathered together and discussed ways to expel the British and the Dutch from Asia, the need for controlling China for the security of Japan, and other such aggressive ideas. On the boat everyone was a patriot and all the Japanese behaved as if they were united in the name of the emperor. Kaneko felt, as he later wrote in his *A History of Despair* (*Zetsubō no seishin shi*), that he was different; he was lonely.[8] He saw in those Japanese representatives of the small people who were nurtured in the damp, secluded, backward lands of Japan. In Kaneko's eye, they were narrow-minded yet arrogant, looking accomplished yet greedy, appearing determined yet changeable, and honest yet cunning. Kaneko doubted that he was fortunate to have been born Japanese. Watching the waves of the ocean, he was glad that he had left Japan.

When the ship stopped at Singapore, Kaneko was invited by the manager of the prostitutes, with whom he had become friendly on the ship, to stay at his inn. The old man Suzuki was not happy, but Kaneko accepted the invitation. At the inn he met more women and their customers, mostly Malaysian, Chinese, and Indian, and heard about many Japanese, including ex-prisoners and deserters of the Sino-Japanese and Russo-Japanese Wars, who roamed Southeast Asia. Kaneko learned that there were ghostlike people who, because of the Japanese sense of shame and honor, were unable to return to their native land. He saw the hidden effect of the wars, realizing the remnants of the old Japanese ethics actually haunting the Malaysian jungle.[9]

The S.S. *Sado* arrived in Liverpool about a month later. Suzuki and Kaneko took a night train for London and settled in a boardinghouse near the British Museum. Kaneko was annoyed by the constant nagging of Suzuki, but he was grateful for having been introduced to art and antiques. In fact, he was quite amazed by the old man's knowledge of art and ability to appreciate it. Through Suzuki, Kaneko met many dealers and actually attended auctions. It may be that Suzuki hoped to train Kaneko as his business successor, but this discerning old man soon found out that Kaneko possessed little apptitude to be a merchant. In May 1920, therefore, he took Kaneko to his old friend, named Ivan Lepage, in Brussels, Belgium, and made an arrangement whereby Lepage could make repayment of an old debt directly to Kaneko, so that Kaneko, if he preferred it to going to France with Suzuki, could stay in Belgium.

This was how "the most worthwhile, the most memorable period in the entire life" of Kaneko began. He rented a room on the second floor of a café not far from the Lepage house. He had time to read, take walks, and write. One of his favorite places to visit was the Brussels Museum, which housed, among others, paintings by the Brueghels and Hieronymus Bosch. Michael, as depicted in *La chute des anges rebelles* by Brueghel, was fighting the thousands of rebels who looked like a cross between humans and fish. His face was pale, his body leaning forward. Around him, some fishmongers were lying dead, with their slimy bellies up and their ugly toothless mouths open. A naked man without his head was crushed, still in the position of the sex act, under armor and something like a musical instrument, and a huge bird with moth's wings was writhing, caught by the tail of something like a serpent. It was dusk, yet more fish and giant insects were swarming in to join battle. All seemed to Kaneko precise representations of various vices in life. The grotesque creatures so realistically resembled the people he knew: prostitutes, mining engineers, foster parents, and his real father, who had virtually extorted money from him. Kaneko realized that beneath the surface of all things there could be a totally different picture, that reality is deceptive and a "little snake" would have little chance to survive. In his room, Kaneko read poems, including those by Émile Verhaeren, Albert Samain, and Baudelaire, and wrote poems. He felt that he had finally escaped the debauched life he had led in Japan. As his poems accumulated, he knew he must return to Japan.

In November 1920 Kaneko visited Paris. He wanted to see the famous city before he went back to Japan. But Paris was foggy, gloomy, and looked aged, compared with Brussels under the bright summer sun. The historical monuments and artifacts in the city looked to him decayed, chronically fatigued, and tragically bound by fetters. Only the paintings, especially the colorful world of the mysticism of Gustave Moreau, attracted Kaneko. He noticed interesting similarities between Bosch and Moreau and wondered if he could write poetry of concentrated beauty as colorful and evocative as their paintings. He hoped to create meticulous crevices in his poetry so that he could instill in them as many varied aspects of life as he had experienced. After he returned to his hotel room from museums, he worked on his poems.

In December Kaneko boarded a Japanese ship in London. He had not seen any Japanese for some time. Feeling suddenly at home, he talked to Japanese passengers. But the passengers, consisting of magicians, a fruit dealer, a student who apparently was going insane, and a university professor, did not inspire him. Off-duty sailors invited him to gamble. Kaneko recalled his creative life in Brussels and Paris.

One night, while the ship was passing the Indian Ocean, he was struck by a beautiful reflection of the moon on water. Millions of waves seemed to be luring him. He recited to the sea some poems he had been polishing. He was exalted in his youthful thought that he was now in the vanguard, when he thought he heard a roar of applause at his back. The Muses beckoned him: he threw half of the manuscripts he was carrying into the enticing sea.[10] A sailor, also crazed by the moon, tossed his kitten into the sea.

Kaneko returned to Japan in January 1921 and was greeted by the same group of people who had seen him off about a year before. Fukushi, who had organized the farewell party for him, came to see him, accompanied by a young student named Satō Hachirō (1903-1973), the son of a well-known man of letters, Satō Kōroku (1874-1949). Fukushi, now patronized by Satō Kōroku, had published a collection of his poems and was beginning to be recognized by critics. Satō Hachirō had ambitions to become a famous poet. Everyone wanted to hear from Kaneko about poetry in Europe.

The year 1921 was the fiftieth birthday of Shimazaki. Commemorating Shimazaki's achievement in poetry, the Society for Poetic Dialogues (*Shiwakai*), to which most of Kaneko's friends belonged, compiled a collection of poems entitled *The Selected Works of Modern Poets* (*Gendai shijin senshū*). The poets in Japan had so increased in number that such a compilation was considered justifiable, but the actual work of anthologizing such a book involved a risk due to factionalism. The publication of *The Selected Works of Modern Poets* resulted in dissatisfaction and even antagonism in some sectors of the Society. Times had changed: Romanticism in Shimazaki's *shintaishi* was no longer appreciated; yet a large number of the members were opposed to expressing any political thoughts in their work and withdrew from the group to form a new society. Those who remained in the original group retained the name *Shiwakai*, consolidated themselves, and decided to publish a journal.

This journal was the *Japanese Poet* (*Nihon shijin*), which was initially edited by Momota Sōji (1893-1955), a man who had been known as a "democratic" poet because of certain visible influences of Whitman and because of the social consciousness manifested in his works. Kaneko was asked to assist Momota in editing the *Japanese Poet*. Behind this was the influence of Fukushi, who wanted the control of the journal and later actually became the editor of it. With the instinct of an artist Kaneko knew that he should not be involved in factionalism. It was urgent for him to publish his works and to write more. He submitted his poems to the more established journal *Mankind* (*Ningen*), while contributing to Momota's journal only illustrations and short essays on French poetry. *Mankind* published two of Kaneko's poems in October, at the same time that Momota managed to publish the first number of the *Japanese Poet*.

Nevertheless, Kaneko found himself assisting Fukushi to launch his journal called *Paradise* (*Rakuen*) at the end of 1921. He had heard that Fukushi was planning to do this for a long time. Some friends informed Kaneko that Fukushi had several times in the past spent for private purposes the money he had gathered for a proposed journal. Perhaps Kaneko still esteemed Fukushi's earlier activities as a critic of Kitahara, Miki, and other "Symbolists." At any rate, with Kaneko's name as editor, *Paradise* was published three times in 1922. Young Satō was an earnest contributor. Kunikida Torao, the son of the famous novelist Kunikida Doppo (1871-1908), was also a contributor. Kaneko did not dislike his work as editor, but he was concerned with his own poems which he had brought back from Europe. He wanted to publish them as a book. In March 1922, therefore, he confined himself in a temple in Kyoto in order to polish the manuscript for publication and, confident that he had created the world of sublime beauty emitting color and brilliance like those of Moreau, he entitled the book *A May Beetle* (*Koganemushi*).

In July 1923 *A May Beetle* was published in Tokyo by Shin-chōsha, the editor of which he had met earlier at the archery club. In the preface, Kaneko wrote in ornate language:

February 1919. My trip to Europe served as a dissection of the "tumor" which had been growing within me. With it, I, in good time, recovered from my "idleness." [While in Europe] I really enjoyed the refreshing effect of being "aimless". . . . I regained my naiveté, bold-ness and youth, which I had not thought possible, and I devoted my-self to completing my portrait. . . . At any rate, with that as a turning point, I began to be able to understand my character and tastes. After nearly ten years of search, random experiments and a period of Sturm und Drang, I have finally reached the stage in which I can enjoy "appreciating" art. . . . Through writing these poems, I myself dis-covered such a drastic change took place within me. The "revelation" of a new spirit and form is indeed capable of dazzling the artist.[11]

A May Beetle is filled with difficult words and ambiguous expressions. Some poems contain so many Chinese character-compounds that they look like translated Chinese poems. Each word in the book is probably meant to be a jewel that decorated the mystical world of Moreau, and flowery expressions are probably those which bloomed in the poet's mind as fantasized in the field of Flanders. Composed at leisure in Brussels and polished in a Buddhist temple, these poems are detached from reality and their aesthetic principle seems concerned mainly with the external or structural. And decorative as they are, they are heavy reading. The frequently used refrains are mostly ineffective, though some help to amplify the melancholic tone. All these features sharply contrasted with contemporary Japanese poetry, in which message-carrying "democratic" poems—easy-to-sing, easy-to-understand poems for the people and of the people—were popular.

The poet Satō Sōnosuke (1890-1942) wrote an understanding essay on Kaneko for *A May Beetle*, from which the following quotation is taken:

His poetry reminds us of the tapestry woven by the Gobelins, its color reddish, and its feel a little coarse. Besides, its smell—it is like a certain tropical fever or a wild animal. Furthermore, his poetry emits a strange radiance, the glow of the artistry of Babylon. It may be said that the poetry of Kaneko embodies all the sensuous pleasures of Baudelaire, the richness of Rubens, the medieval dreams of the Flemish painters.[12]

The opening poem of *A May Beetle* is entitled "Cloud" (*"Kumo"*), which begins with:

> A proud jockey in the blue sky
> From far, shaking the distant bronze woods
> As arrogant as a king
> Crosses the border and the platinum mountains
>
> Tell me a story glorified in your heart
> About the pain chronicled in your breast[13]

In the latter half of this poem the distinction between the cloud and the listener is blurred and, in the end, it is the poet who is seen off to the sky "by the season."

One of the simplest poems in terms of form and diction is "Passages" ("*Shōku*"), which may be taken as vignettes containing portraits of the poet.

B.   A rosy smile appearing between the branches of a tree
    A form that elegantly passes through the scattered reeds

    In the fragrant woods before the moon rises
    I roam around the lake with a maiden's wish

E.   The town decorated with rosy snow
    A lonely window wet in sleet
    My cheeks are smudged day after day

    The quickening sun at dusk in Europe
    A canary in a cage crying as faintly as her life

F.   A fallen leaf meditates in rapture
    A fallen leaf breathes like a wounded finch

    A fallen leaf longs for the blue sky
    A fallen leaf longs for the blue sky[14]

The poet seems to be feeling merely lonely. He is narcissistic, having retreated from the stage of the "little snake" of *The House of Earthen Walls*. *A May Beetle* did not make any significant impact on contemporary Japanese poetry.

Much of the attention of the poetic world of Japan was on Hagiwara Sakutarō (1886-1942), who had just published his second successful collection of poems, *The Blue Cat* (*Aoneko*). In fact, Hagiwara had been enjoying a high reputation as a master of diction and a creator of a unique world of melancholy, even haunted, yet lyrical beauty, since he had published his first book in 1917. Hagiwara's language was ordinary, but it was finely tuned to a sensuous musical effect, curiously matching the poet's pessimistic visions of life. Compared with the work of either Hagiwara or the "democratic" poets, Kaneko's *A May Beetle* was very different in both content and outlook.

The other part of Satō Sōnosuke's 1923 remarks on Kaneko may be quoted, to conclude:

Kaneko has yet to grow. His diction seems to need more refinement. However, he definitely has qualities; he has potential. It is to be hoped that his rapture, his joy, his sorrow, and his dedication will come to full maturity. His world will develop with each of his subsequent volumes of verse.[15]

CHAPTER 2

"The Song of Wandering": *1924-1932*

THE Great Kanto Earthquake that hit the Tokyo area shortly before noon, September 1, 1923, destroyed not only many buildings from the previous era, but also the institutions and order that the Japanese had established. Tokyo burned like an inferno. After-tremors were frequent, and the casualties reached more than 100,000. The social, economic and political effects of the quake were far-reaching. There were rumors that the water was poisoned and that whatever properties remained were being looted. There was also an excessive concern about possible uprisings of the leftists and Koreans, and the police were reported to be overtly active. Apparently some people were taking advantage of this confusion to subdue the Marxists and anarchists who had been increasing their influence. As a result, many "self-defense" groups were organized, and bloody conflicts occurred in the ruined city.

That afternoon Kaneko managed to go to Sumi's house and brought her out to the large garden of a nearby house which seemed the safest spot within their reach. There were already many other refugees taking shelter in the garden. Rescue was slow to come and demagoguery reigned. After spending several sleepless nights, the refugees grew wild. Kaneko was brought before some "self-defense" people and accused of being a Socialist. He knew the reason: he had organized a group in the garden and demanded that the proprietor allow them to continue their stay on his premises. One bully clubbed him, calling, "Down with you, Socialist!" Kaneko sustained cuts and bruises on his head and left thumb. He realized what had been happening in the world of thought in Japan. His feeling of evanescence was combined with a deep

38

sense of distrust in man and doubts about his own ideological stand.

Kaneko escaped from Tokyo. He carried with him one book, *Max Stirner's The Ego and His Own (Der Einzige und sein Eigentum)*. Translated into Japanese as *Jigakyō* or "the canon for the self" by renowned anarchist Tsuji Jun (1885-1944), the book had been favorably accepted as a sort of "canon" by Japanese intellectuals. For the kind of intellectuals who were dissatisfied with established thoughts and institutions, Stirner's manifesto, "All things are meaningless to the Self," was appealing. Kaneko found tne book's theme very appropriate for the occasion and thought that he would agree to Stirner's nihilistic view of all things. Having just witnessed the crumbling of the city of Tokyo, he could not think any concept or value really substantial. Were not even God and Buddha simply images? Had not justice and freedom also turned out to be nonexistent, like a mirage? Kaneko knew that his art, his concept of beauty, was shaken. He realized that Moreau's color and fancy, the world of *A May Beetle*, was buried in the ruins.

Kaneko stopped at Nagoya. He did not quite remember Nagoya, where he had lived as a boy, but he had met an admirer from that city, named Makino Katsuhiko. Through Makino, he was introduced to some local poets and was treated courteously as a poet from Tokyo. He was even asked to give a public lecture on poetry together with the famous poet (Yone) Noguchi Yonejirō (1875-1947), who had returned to his native town from a lecture tour to England. Neither Noguchi's lecture, which used candle lights for effect, nor Kaneko's, which showed his lack of preparation, was well received by the audience. Nevertheless, he was paid an honorarium with which he bought a train ticket to Nishinomiya, farther away from Tokyo. In Nishinomiya, a city facing the Seto Inland Sea, Kaneko's sister Sute was married and well-to-do. Kaneko killed time there, visiting a small shipyard and harbor nearby. He wrote some poems which he later included in *The Faltering (Mizu no rurō)*, published in 1926. No one ever even dreamed at that time that twenty years later Kaneko would come to live with Sute's family in a remote province in order to escape the air raids on Tokyo.

Kaneko returned to Tokyo with financial assistance extended by Satō Kōroku, who was living not far from Nishinomiya. He settled in the same house as before, which had somehow escaped destruction. It was the beginning of 1924. A little later, Makino came to Tokyo from Nagoya and joined the circle of Kaneko's "friends." It was this Makino, a somewhat officious man, who introduced Kaneko to a young girl who, within four months, became his bride.

The girl was Mori Michiyo, the eldest of the four children of the Mori family in Mie. The pride and hope of not only her family, but also of the Mie Prefecture, she was a student sent by the Prefecture to Japan's highest educational institution for women, Tokyo Women's Normal College, where she had an excellent academic record. Like many educated women, she had read A Doll's House, was sympathetic toward Nora, talked about women's suffrage and emancipation, and wrote poems. Furthermore, she had a lover, a student of Tokyo University, with whom she was having problems.

Michiyo learned that her girl friend's lover, named Ōyama Hiromitsu, belonged to the circle of the Paradise, the journal that Kaneko had edited for Fukushi in 1922. She became very interested in Kaneko's circle, which included such young men as Ōyama, Makino, Kunikida, and Satō Hachirō. An agressive woman, Michiyo made an appointment with Kaneko through Ōyama and Makino in the hope that she might perhaps be given a chance to make a debut in the literary world and to consult with Kaneko about her personal problems. For Michiyo, Kaneko was a rising star in the "professional" literary world, having edited journals, published books, and studied abroad. In still-smoldering Tokyo, showing the ugly scars of the disaster everywhere, Kaneko met Michiyo, who came wearing a uniform of the college. The meeting of the two was melodramatic and almost fated. They immediately fell in "love" and developed relations—the relations which remained indissoluble until 1975. Only a few months after they met, one morning at the beginning of July 1924, Michiyo came from her dormitory to Kaneko's house, as she had been in the habit of doing, and whispered in his ear that she was pregnant.

There were two more opportunities: Kaneko received an advance payment from Shinchōsha for his proposed collection of poems, The Faltering; he also received Fukushi's invitation to visit Hirosaki, a northern city where he had moved. Taking advantage of this good fortune Kaneko went with Michiyo to Hirosaki. During their stay that lasted about a month, Tomita Saika (1890-), one of the "democratic" poets, visited them with his wife. Tomita, eccentric in private life, was a founding member of the Society for Poetic Dialogue and was well known as a translator of Edward Carpenter and Walt Whitman. The three couples were together day and night, spending lavishly and talking loudly. Naturally, their unrestrained behavior was frowned upon by the conservative local residents. Kaneko thought, however, that he was able to broaden his knowledge of poetry and awareness of social thoughts through conversations with Fukushi and Tomita.

When Kaneko and Michiyo returned to Tokyo, they were informed by Michiyo's classmate that Tokyo Women's Normal College was preparing to take disciplinary action against Michiyo. By telegram Michiyo summoned her father to Tokyo. Michiyo's father arranged with the college for Michiyo's withdrawal from school for reasons of health, and Kaneko became the father of a son, Ken. Now the most urgent matter was finance. Neither Kaneko nor Michiyo was prepared for family life. Kaneko had used up Sōtarō's legacy to help his father and brother, in unsuccessful investments, for his own pleasures, for traveling, for treating his friends, and for publishing journals and books. Michiyo could not get monetary support from her father, a schoolteacher at that time.

Kaneko visited newspaper and magazine publishers and tried to sell his poems. However, the majority of the editors and publishers did not even recognize Kaneko's name, while a few remembered him as a minor poet who wrote stylish but empty poems. The publishing firms, many still trying to recover from the shock of the earthquake, had not forgotten the quick rise and decline of some literary movements in Japan. They remembered well how the popularity of writers and their sales had fluctuated in the past, forcing many firms to declare bankruptcy. Understandably, they were generally apathetic toward poetry, while they favored prose, particularly popular fiction. Kaneko managed to get hold of a small publisher through connections and received money in installments for his translations of French poems. Yet, he could not pay the rent for a small house and moved to a two-room apartment with a tin roof. Then, unable to stand the heat in the apartment, he moved to another small rented house. In his attempt to earn money, Kaneko was half-knowingly tricked into translating for nothing Maurice Leblanc's story of Arsène Lupin for a publisher named Kōgyokudō. Because of his pride as the author of *The House of Earthen Walls* and *A May Beetle*, he used an entirely new pen name, Kurobe Takehiko. In the meantime, he borrowed as much money as possible from his friends and sold whatever he possibly could. Many of his "friends" abandoned him and his "circle" disappeared. Even loyal Makino, who had admired Kaneko as a teacher and introduced him to Michiyo, left him. His relatives were disgusted with his bohemian life, his landlords were angry, and his creditors were dumbfounded.

Perhaps because of irregular life and inadequate nutrition, Ken became sick, refusing to accept milk. Michiyo had no choice but to ask her parents for help in order to take care of him. Since Michiyo's parents had moved to Nagasaki, a port in the western end of Japan, Kaneko and Michiyo traveled to Nagasaki by a boat sailing from Yokohama to Europe. Whatever the reason and the method, it was what the Japanese scornfully called *"miyakoochi,"* or "being cast from the capital." Feeling defeated and ashamed, Kaneko feared that he might be permanently outcast, unable to return to "the capital." During about five months' stay with Michiyo's parents, therefore, Kaneko managed to go to Tokyo a few times in order to keep in touch with "friends," "publishers," and "the world of letters." Satō Kōroku assisted him again by letting him write an essay for the *Mainichi* paper in his name, and paid him 100 yen.

There was only a brief period in which Kaneko could feel triumphant as a victor of love. Although he previously had not heard of the young man with whom Michiyo had had problems, he began to hear of him. He also noticed a certain shadow overcasting Michiyo's mind and behavior. Furthermore, he thought he saw an incident which caused him to suspect Michiyo's fidelity. Added to his financial problems, this was a shattering blow to Kaneko. He needed to dispel his despair: he decided to use the 100 yen from Satō Kōroku for a trip to Shanghai, the nearest foreign port from Nagasaki. He had a memory of the Chinese city, where his boat had stopped once.

The city's air of intrigue and corruption, its smell of cooking oil and raw scallions, its dirty streets, rickshaws, and pimps all seemed very appropriate to Kaneko's state of mind. The novelist Tanizaki Jun'ichirō (1886-1965), who had been living near Nishinomiya since the earthquake, wrote several letters of introduction for Kaneko to influential Chinese men of letters, including Lu-hsün (1881-1936), Kuo Mo-jo (1892-), T'ien Han (1898-), and Yü Ta-fu (1896-1945). During their short stay in Shanghai, Kaneko and Michiyo were able to forget, temporarily, the troubles of life in Japan. They met all those to whom Tanizaki had written introductions, except Kuo, and were courteously treated.

Kaneko wrote poems, but, unable to completely dispel the feeling of defeat, he could not concentrate. Besides, he was not certain about his old thought and aesthetics. He searched his soul, and groped for a new style. The poems he wrote in those days reflected the desolate state of his mind, while they indicated that Kaneko began to cast off *A May Beetle*'s narcissism. Here are the opening lines of a poem called "A Vortex" (*"Uzu"*).

> Shanghai is a blender
> All men are mixed.
>
> Shanghai is a messy drawer
> Death too is in it.
>
> It is hard to be chaste. In Shanghai
> No such word as chastity exists.
>
> But Shanghai is no more unusual
> Than any other boring city.
> Only it is dustier.
>
> Shanghai is for both
> Those who need money for tickets
> And those who need tickets for money.[1]

Back in Tokyo, Kaneko visited his acquaintances, asking for an advance subscription fee of one yen per copy for a proposed book of poems. The book, *The Sharks Dive (Fuka shizumu)*, was co-authored by Kaneko and Michiyo in the hope to unite the couple. It was a thin book, and when he delivered it to those who had subscribed, some complained of its high price. Kaneko failed to make money, and again went into debt. He moved several times, at night, after having accumulated unpaid bills. He no longer had any furniture to move with him. As his last resort, Kaneko asked his brother for help. His brother, once engaged in some unlawful enterprises like selling dubious merchandise and counterfeiting in the mountains in Korea, was settled in Tokyo with an ex-geisha at the time. The brother's advice was that he should run away by night, which Kaneko had already done several times.

It was already the end of 1926 when Shinchōsha finally published *The Faltering*, for which Kaneko had received an advance payment before he married Michiyo. The book was in the series called *The Modern Poets (Gendai shijin sōsho)*, which included such well-known poets as Noguchi, Kawaji, Miki, and Hagiwara. Satō Sōnosuke, who had written a tribute for *A May Beetle*, and Momota, who edited the *Japanese Poet*, were also given a volume as "modern poets" in the series. These "democratic" and lyricist poets, however, were being challenged by Dadaist and anarchist poets, who accustomed the reader to expect unconventional styles and to relish abstruse or destructive ideas. Some ambitious writers were intent upon creating shocking effects in literature. Despite high hopes and sheer need for money, *The Faltering* did not sell, so that Kaneko was obliged to sell the leftover copies to a second-hand bookstore at bulk rates.

The Faltering contained about thirty poems that Kaneko had written after the Great Kanto Earthquake. Some were sketches he had made while he stayed with Sute's family in Nishinomiya. Some were prose poems. None was shocking; most were "faltering," so to speak, in both form and content. Water and travel on water were the main subjects, and the dominant theme was the poet's longing for an indefinable something, or his lament for passing youth and unattainable poetry. One poem that was to represent this collection and remained prominent among all his works is "The Song of Wandering" ("*Hyōhaku no uta*").

The Song of Wandering

I turn a dusty globe,
As my dreams go, round the countries.

A cosmic breath crossing people, race and nation:
A line of sadness piercing time and matter.

Ill luck to grow old still dreaming:
Avoiding duties, gaining little from life,
Unsatisfied, slipping through women's arms,
I was excited—only by the lure of travel.

Ah, my passion for coloring books in earlier days.
Drawn by sweeter, richer and more distant life, rare trees and herbs
    from an unknown land.
Parrots, pineapples, palms, black monkeys with long tails and
    beady-eye.
The yellow and red lust of a tiger
Crushing bamboo in the steamy rain.

A balloon disappearing into the sky above a port.
Evening tides tapping the pillars of a rotten pier.
A bottomless barrel sways red
In bits of straw and jellyfish.

A gong's dong at departure.
A flock of seagulls screaming at waterbreak.
The anchor on a pulled-up cable
Looks smaller than a tattoo on the arm. Already
The ship is out to sea.

The smell of water penetrates the core
The root of grief in the heart
The cold belly of an old fish
Lying on the weathered board.

Wandering tells me, leaning softly,
"A permanent residence is also a journey."
Before I know it, while still in bed,
I roam in the midst of an ocean.

The harshness of waves' yellow bowels
Smearing the windows of a third-class cabin.
Of wintry sky in a foreign land
Hovering above the skylight of an attic room.

For the stupidity of yearning
My greed for dreams
Chasing a mirage, my heart is empty
Nothing to hold on to.

My youth passes, alas,
Wandering, I know nothing else.
Leaning against a park fence, standing on a rooftop deck,
I call out to the setting sun for the happiness I never had.
Pride, love, all the dreams of my youth!

A picnic with black Spanish umbrellas.
Wooden horses. Liliom. Momentary glory of fireworks.
Golden haze. Fragrance of ashes.
Who in the world is happy today?

My love, friend, or parents? For whom
Is this straight, arrow-like longing?
I don't know. But I would bet my life's earnings,
My share of luck, on this moment of youth.
Shall I decorate my dingy room
Like a flagship in a ceremony?
Gaiety of life slowly receding!

At night I bury my face in fading flowers,
Listen to my 29th year pulsing away
Against a sporadic melody from a distant theater.
Ah, what is this burning irritation in my life?[2]

To Kaneko the poems of Hagiwara looked as though they
relied only on feeling. He wondered if Hagiwara merely
created in his head the illusion of melancholy, as many
Japanese intellectuals did at the time, under the spell of Edgar
Allan Poe, perhaps? A mere feeling would have little significance in life, no matter how noble or precious it might be,
Kaneko thought, unless it were rooted in a certain place at a
certain time in a certain period. Might a poem be like a display
of fireworks against the darkness? If it had no connection with
the tremendous accumulation of man's joy or pain or the glory
or sorrow yet to come, poetry might be the same as a mirage,
Kaneko speculated. However, the period was beginning to
turn into a period of "feeling." Kawabata Yasunari (1899-1972),
the Nobel Laureate of 1968, Yokomitsu Riichi (1898-1947), and
other writers had formed a school called the School of New
Feeling (*Shin kankaku ha*). Through their journal the *Literary
Age* (*Bungei jidai*), the New Feeling writers opposed particularly the proletarian writers who published their works in the
Literary Front (*Bungei sensen*), and they advocated the use of
imagery derived from the author's immediate "feeling" rather

than from analytical observation or prescribed thought. Kaneko was skeptical about the overt reliance on either feeling or political ideology. He was convinced that one's Self could be cultivated only through one's own thinking and doing, "the core" of life, "the root of grief in one's heart." Writing "The Song of Wandering," Kaneko knew what "the burning irritation" in his heart was. It was poetry. He determined that he would wager his "life's earning," his "share of luck for this moment of youth." He had dedicated *The Faltering* to Satō Kōroku, Fukushi, Michiyo, and Sumi.

The conditions in the publishing world in Japan changed in the meantime. In fact, the publishing business in Japan was suddenly experiencing unprecedented prosperity due mainly to the success of two large publishing firms, Kaizōsha and Shunyōdō, which published collections of modern Japanese literary works at the popular price of one yen a volume. Sales were so good and novelists and their beneficiaries were paid so well that journalism called it the "one-yen book boom." Many writers built new houses, while others traveled abroad. But this "one-yen book boom" did not benefit Kaneko. Among the writers who benefited from this boom, Yokomitsu was sympathetic to poets and extended his help to Kaneko. He gave Kaneko some piecework for the prosperous publishers, which included Kaizōsha and Kōdansha. However, even with Yokomitsu's introduction Kaneko had to wait in the waiting room of the publisher for a turn to talk to the editor. Fashionable novelists occasionally walked in, and they ignored others' appointments. Inspired by such incidents, Kaneko wrote a novel which was based on his trip to Shanghai and submitted it to Kaizōsha for a contest prize. He had asked Yokomitsu and Satō Haruo (1892-1964), a writer who was highly successful in both poetry and the novel, to evaluate it. Both Yokomitsu and Satō Haruo assured Kaneko that the novel would have a good chance to win the prize, but Kaneko did not win it.

Just then he saw Kunikida, who was looking for some effective way to spend the money paid for his father's novels. Kaneko persuaded Kunikida to go abroad and, leaving Michiyo in Tokyo, he again left Japan in March 1927, with Kunikida. While they were in Shanghai, Yokomitsu came. They visited Chinese bathhouses and restaurants and went to the race track to spend money and time.

The moment Kaneko stepped down from his ship onto the

pier at Nagasaki, he felt an ominous sensation within him. His instinct told him that Michiyo had definitely left him. He picked up Ken at his in-laws' house and together they hurried to Tokyo. Sure enough, Michiyo was not at home. It was dark, and the air in the May evening was almost motionless. The last train had left hours before, and there was no sign that Michiyo would return that night. The next morning Kaneko left Ken at the house of Sute, who had moved to Tokyo from Nishinomiya, and called on his neighbor Kusano Shimpei (1903-   ) for help. Kusano, a poet who was managing a little mimeographed magazine at that time, knew what had happened. He took Kaneko to a house where Michiyo was living with her student lover. By the house there was a narrow, dirty ditch. Kaneko waited, pacing along the ditch, until Kusano, Michiyo, and her lover came out of the house. In order to conceal his awkwardness, Kaneko talked to the student. The lover did not answer.

What we perceive through ear and eye is only one tenth of the reality at a particular time and place. It is merely a passing impression that is deceptive and misleading. Yet we believe it to be the reality. The truth is that we are always cheated: we have a misconception that reality never cheats us, and we try to give a show of truth by forcing ourselves to adjust to the reality. Most of our daily worries come from this.[3]

Adultery was a criminal offense in Japan: a husband would sue his wife, though a wife was not allowed to take any action against her unfaithful husband. Kaneko's friends who expected more gossip were puzzled to see that Kaneko was behaving as if he were indifferent to Michiyo's affair. But what could any law, whether feudal or modern, do about the humiliation of a man who was feeling completely defeated? What could it do for his pride? Besides, Kaneko needed Michiyo, and he told her that they should have a cooling-off period. They moved again, this time to a small room on the second floor of a cheap eel restaurant, and tried to rekindle their love. However, because of their convenient location and the "fame" that the affair had created among their acquaintances, they began receiving an increased number of "friends." The friends and Kaneko talked about the current rise of Communist writers and the death of Akutagawa Ryūnosuke (1892-1927). There were reports that the artistic writer Akutagawa killed himself because he thought he had lost his stand to leftist writers' advances in the literary world, and some predicted that more suicides like Akutagawa would appear. Meanwhile, Michiyo continued to see her lover, and Kaneko dodged the creditors, who included the owner of the little restaurant downstairs.

On one of those days, Kaneko went to the publisher Kōdansha, from which he hoped to obtain some piecework. While he was waiting in the lobby for his turn to see a manager, he met Okamoto Jun (1901-   ), an anarchist poet, who was also paying a visit to the publisher in order to get some work. They recognized each other and talked, lamenting the times and their lots. As they left Kōdansha, Kaneko took Okamoto to his apartment and together with Michiyo they went out to bars. Kaneko had stopped drinking, but Michiyo drank a good deal. So did Okamoto, and he missed the last train home. Kaneko then took him back to his apartment again, but there were only enough quilts to sleep two people, and Michiyo slept in one. According to Okamoto's recollection, Kaneko told Okamoto to sleep in the same quilt with Michiyo, and Okamoto counter-offered that Michiyo alone sleep and both men stay up, to which Kaneko agreed.[4] At an eerie time of night, Kaneko fetched a sketch book and demonstrated to Okamoto his skill in drawing erotic pictures. Okamoto thought that some of the pictures were masochistic: he did not recognize that the picture of a bleeding, naked woman was taken from Bosch, who had fascinated Kaneko earlier; he thought that the woman was Michiyo. Kaneko's heart was devastated, but the poet was seeing something, the object called man. To him, man seemed reducible to a single thing: the act he used to see in the old picture books in the earthen-walled warehouse of his house. He could now draw similar, but far more realistic, pictures with ease. It was this man with whom Kaneko was preoccupied. Poems, whether they were by "Symbolists," "lyricists," "anarchists," or "proletarians," appeared to him to lack the profundity hidden in life itself.

Kaneko's situation was such that the faster they moved out of the apartment above the eel restaurant and got out of Tokyo, the more chance there would be for them to regain their humanity. Kaneko decided to get out of Japan.

> Ill luck to grow old still dreaming:
> Avoiding duties, gaining little from life,

Unsatisfied, slipping through women's arms,
I was excited—only by the lure of travel.

In September 1928 Kaneko left Tokyo with Michiyo, stop-
ping at Nagoya and then Osaka due to lack of money. In Osaka
Kaneko contacted Masaoka Iruru (1904-1958), a former literature enthusiast and admirer of *A May Beetle*, and an eccentric
apprentice of an Osaka comic. Through Masaoka's introduction, Kaneko at one time appeared on a radio talk show; at
another he helped Masaoka sell his work to a newspaper and
received some compensation. Dragging along Michiyo, who
obviously was unable to forget her lover, Kaneko was a desperate man. He would vacantly watch the dark streets of
Osaka, and murmur lines he remembered from Baudelaire.
Finally, Kaneko visited Tanizaki, the novelist who in 1925 had
written letters of introduction to Chinese writers for him. He
had just met an art dealer, who slyly suggested that he obtain
famous writers' calligraphy and signatures for quick money. At
the Tanizaki house, Kaneko was given some calligraphy which
Tanizaki produced for him and, on his way back he almost fell
unconscious on a railroad track. He had forced himself to drink
saké in order to get rid of his shame. At the end of November,
Kaneko and Michiyo arrived in Nagasaki.

Shanghai greeted the couple, who had neither purpose nor
hope. As before, the city was overpopulated, its streets chaotic, fitting the state of mind of the visitors. An old landlady in
the north end of the city remembered Kaneko and offered an
apartment. In the back room of the apartment house several
drifters gathered to gamble all day long, and some women sold
their charms. A mixture of all desires and problems, a melting
pot of all races, Shanghai made the *cocu* and his wife forget the
cries of Ken, whom they had left in Nagasaki. Kaneko was only
relieved by the thought that he was at last out of Japan, away
from his creditors and Michiyo's lover. He had only six yen in
his pocket.

In January 1929 it was very cold in Shanghai. Unable to bear
the cold, they would go to a heated bookstore not far from their
apartment. The bookstore was the one managed by Uchiyama
Kanzō (1885-1959), the Japanese who, after the Communist
Revolution of 1949, was honored by the Chinese government
for his contributions to cultural exchange between China and

Japan. At that time Uchiyama's store was serving as a sort of social club for both Chinese and Japanese intellectuals and political refugees. For the Chinese it was the only important supplier of leftist literature, such as works by Kropotkin, Marx, and Engels, and for the Japanese it was a place of informal communication with Chinese progressive writers like Lu-hsün and Yü Ta-fu. To his surprise, Kaneko learned that Uchiyama was netting about 80,000 yen a month.

An idea struck him: Kaneko produced an illustrated pornographic book in mimeograph and had it sold by a Chinese pimp. His enterprise was greeted by Japanese social outcasts, drifters, and sailors in the Shanghai area and brought him money that he badly needed, but the business soon declined as the market was saturated. Kaneko had an ugly fight with the pimp over profit. Just then, a friend named Akita Giichi, from Kaneko's old circle, appeared before him. Akita had become a painter. The next day, Kaneko and Akita were on the other side of the Whangpoo River, trying to sell Akita's paintings to the manager of a Japanese textile mill. They both knew that the paintings were not of high value, but Kaneko rationalized: what difference was there between selling pornography to willing sailors and forcing art on an unwilling buyer? Virtually extorting money from innocent people, Kaneko thought he would not even deserve to be poked by a Chinese boatman if his corpse were discovered floating in the river. The water was polluted, smelling like a rotten animal. Akita, homeless and in the advanced stages of tuberculosis, moved to Kaneko's apartment and used it as his workshop to produce more paintings.

A letter reached them from Japan, and Kaneko learned that Michiyo had been writing to her lover in Tokyo. With a hopeless, self-inflicting vengeance, Kaneko helped Michiyo to print her poems bound in the jacket design that her lover had sent her. The thin book, printed with the aid of Uchiyama, featured Michiyo's love poem entitled "My Heart Turned to Cinders" ("*Kōkusu ni natta shinzō*"). Maedakō Hiroichirō (1888-1957), the popular Socialist writer and a translator of Upton Sinclair's *The Jungle*, who was leading a very debauched life in Shanghai on a Kaizōsha expense account, commented that Kaneko and Michiyo were being treated too well by the worthless people who surrounded them. He took

Kaneko and Michiyo to bars and dance halls, and advised that
they should join the Communist party. Perhaps Maedakō was
disgusted with the government's suppression of the leftist
literary movement in which he had been involved back in Japan. It was Lu-hsün who really worried about Kaneko and politely asked him if his sojourn in Shanghai was not becoming
unnecessarily long. One day when Kaneko was walking outside of the International Settlement, he was surrounded by
toughs and shot at. It was high time for him to leave Shanghai.

Is it Paris, London, Lisbon or Milan? Wherever our destination is, we
end up finding less than we expected; and we adjust our dreams to
avoid disappointment. Only the unreliability of our dreams is constant. But isn't this constancy man's instability, the nonexistent arrow
pointing to the key that promises man eternity? To Madrid, to the
Cape of Good Hope; we swear in dreams and we are deceived in
reality. Tell me, God. Where can we go?[5]

In mid-June 1929 Kaneko and Michiyo appeared in Singapore. They had spent more than a month in Hong Kong, selling Kaneko's drawings to raise funds enough to continue their
journey. Kaneko told Michiyo that Hong Kong would be the
last port from which she could go back to her lover in Tokyo.
Michiyo sobbed, and no more letters arrived from her lover.

In Singapore there were many varieties of people, including
Japanese, Chinese, Indians, and Malaysians, and the difference between the rich and the poor was striking. However, the
scorching sun seemed to numb the suffering of the deprived
people. It was lucky for Kaneko that the Japanese newspapers
in Singapore and Java extended their sympathy and aid to enable him to continue his journey. Fighting against incredible
heat, Kaneko and Michiyo traveled and saw huge plantations
dotted with Dutch mansions, modern bridges in the old vil-
lages, and good roads in the undeveloped fields of palms and
banana trees. At one place, they saw the dry head of a man
who had plotted to kill a wealthy Dutch merchant, still stuck
on a spear. Often they heard the cries of giant lizards. The
Japanese on those islands, mostly rubber planters and mining
engineers, were hungry for news and welcomed Kaneko's visit
and bought his paintings. Many wanted him to paint family
portraits like photographs. With the money, which was barely
enough for one boat ticket to Europe, Kaneko decided to send
Michiyo to Paris so that he could join her there later. Paris,

however harsh a place it might be, seemed the only destination where they might rekindle their love and hope.

> The smell of water penetrates the core
> The root of grief in the heart
> The cold belly of an old fish
> Lying on the weathered board.

> Wandering tells me, leaning softly,
> "A permanent residence is also a journey."
> Before I know it, while still in bed,
> I roam in the midst of an ocean.

In a berth near the bottom of a ship sailing to the Indian Ocean, Kaneko had a dream: the alligators he saw in a Malaysian village came chasing him, while millions of fish glistened around him. It was a dream of Hieronymus Bosch. Awakened, Kaneko recollected that he walked in a torrential squall and kept walking in the thick steam created by the heat of the sun in Sumatra. He felt a pain on his arm, once terribly swollen because of mosquito bites; he thought he heard the squeaking of bats that darkened the sky of the island he had visited. He remembered the hunger and the heat that exhausted him on a small Chinese boat. The bitter taste of wandering lingered in Kaneko for a long time.

Paris at the end of 1929 was as foggy as it had been about ten years before. First of all, Kaneko had to locate Michiyo. He went to the Japanese embassy and found Michiyo's name and address added at the end of a list of the resident Japanese. In the embassy there were reports that most of the Japanese "artists" in Paris were in financial difficulties and some "ex-artists" were begging on the sidewalks. For Kaneko the world of *La Bohème* did not seem to exist. He hired a cab and hurried to Michiyo's apartment. She was alone. Relieved of his anxiety, he suddenly felt very tired.

Kaneko "tried everything but male prostitution and writing poetry" in order to stay alive together with Michiyo in Paris. The cold wind of Paris seemed capable of separating man and wife, unless they are bonded by both love and money. The job market for foreigners was very small. Some Japanese men were living as "servants" with rich middle-aged French widows or divorcées, and a Kimura offered Kaneko an opportunity to "serve" a wealthy American woman. Those who did not choose such odd jobs would gather at the Suwa Hotel, an old inn managed by an elderly Japanese couple, and wait for Japanese tourists to arrive. Some of these men were pimps. One time-consuming task that Kaneko engaged in for money was to help a Japanese student write a dissertation in French on Japanese agrarian history. Another was to help impoverished Japanese to evade French creditors for a commission. Still another job which was a little more profitable was to compile a Japanese residents' directory. One time, Kaneko visited a Japanese embassy attaché named Kaba and solicited money for the purpose of assisting Japanese students financially troubled in Paris. Kaneko also planned to paint parasols on Trouville beach to sell, but this plan did not materialize because he was unable to obtain a peddler's permit.

Michiyo, in her own nonchalant way, had made many friends, while getting lessons in French and social dance. She had become friendly with an Italian sculptor who used her as a model, a Japanese import-exporter who hired her as a guide, a Frenchman who helped her to translate her poems, and some others. She had also worked as an extra for a French film. Kaneko knew, and Michiyo knew too, that most of the Parisian "friends" had the obvious intention of becoming more than friendly with her. Some openly propositioned her even in Kaneko's presence.

Kaneko walked aimlessly in the city. He was no longer drawn to Musée Gustave Moreau on Rue de la Rochefoucaud. Often he went to the cemetery in Montparnasse and strolled among the graves of Maupassant, Baudelaire, and other famous literary figures. He was forlorn, feeling his pulse quickened because of a small amount of rum he took with coffee. He noticed that his shoes, purchased at a Chinese store in Singapore, were completely worn out.

To be sure, Kaneko lived life in Paris exactly as he had dreamed he would. He trudged in the large city and tried to kill greater pains at heart. His struggle for survival on a daily basis made him forget Michiyo's lover, his "friends," and Ken. He did not write any poems, but he lived poetry, so to speak, as evidenced by the fact that passages from his earlier poem are curiously prophetic.

> For the stupidity of yearning
> My greed for dreams

> Chasing a mirage, my heart is empty
> Nothing to hold on to.
>
> My youth passes, alas,
> Wandering, I know nothing else.
> Leaning against a park fence, standing on a rooftop deck,
> I call out to the setting sun for the happiness I never had.
> Pride, love, all the dreams of my youth!

Kaneko moved from one cheap apartment to another. One day, he stopped at a hotel where he and Michiyo had lived previously. It was a good instinct, because his former landlady handed him a letter, which was addressed to Michiyo from her father and contained 300 *yen*, equivalent to 4,000 *francs*. Kaneko knew that the money was meant to be for a boat ticket to Japan for Michiyo. The thought that he had forced Michiyo to follow him through hardships in Southeast Asia and Paris hurt him. However, he did not tell her about the money. Michiyo, too, he thought, had flirted with other men, forcing him to roam the world.

> Shall I decorate my dingy room
> Like a flagship in a ceremony?
> Gaiety of life slowly receding!

The next morning, Kaneko took Michiyo to women's apparel shops on Rue de l'Opéra and bought her a set of expensive clothes and accessories. He bought a pair of new shoes for himself, too.

Some Japanese lived elegantly in Paris. Fujita (Foujita) Tsuguharu (1886-1968) was already a well-established painter and an object of envy among the Japanese. The woman novelist Okamoto Kanoko (1889-1939) lived in a luxurious apartment on the Seine, taking full advantage of the "one-yen book boom." The poetess Fukao Sumako (1893-1974) was also in Paris. Kaneko visited those people. There was no Gertrude Stein, the patroness of the Lost Generation, for the Japanese, at least not for Kaneko. In contrast to the prosperous writers from Japan, he was now a craftsman, making picture frames for Matsumoto, an art dealer from America. The news about the Japanese literary world these people brought to him had no immediacy for him. His condition was such that he would appreciate a free lunch more than news about Japanese poetry.

When he had no job at all, he called on a Japanese man in Lyon
only to discover that he was a stranger with the same name as
his old acquaintance. Watching the stain on the wall of a hotel,
Kaneko could feel the rotation of the earth. If he committed
suicide, he thought, he would not be noticed by anyone for a
long time and Michiyo would have no trouble finding someone to live with.

In November 1930, time for leaving Paris came when
Michiyo accepted a friend's offer of a job as secretary in the
Belgian port city of Antwerp. Kaneko had no choice but to run
to his old friend Ivan Lepage in Brussels. For about ten
months until he finally left Europe in October 1931, Kaneko
lived like an amoeba in a small room on the second floor of a
laundry shop in Brussels. Unlike an amoeba, however, Kaneko
had no room to stretch: he did not have a tomorrow. The coo-
ing of pigeons outside of his room sounded to him like the
lovers' talk he had heard through the wall of a hotel in Lyon.

Mr. Lepage had not changed. He often invited him to dinner
and entertained him. One weekend Lepage made arrangements so that Michiyo could come to Brussels to meet him and
stay with Kaneko. At that time, Kaneko was suffering from insomnia, because he was unable to rid himself of the suspicion
that Michiyo's job in Antwerp was not exactly "secretarial."
He was tired and only vaguely recollected his youthful
passions as he wrote A May Beetle ten years earlier. Instead of
poems, he again produced some sketches, which Lepage took
pains to sell. That year, foggy Flanders seemed more suitable
to nurture demons than to arouse the spirits of the Parnassian
poets. At the edge of the city where Kaneko strolled, there was
a gypsy circus stranded. He saw there the end of a homeless
troupe, a civilization, and himself. Lepage judged it best that
Kaneko go back to Japan.

Kaneko was resting alone in a café in Paris. It was good to be
back in the familiar city, Kaneko sighed, nursing in his mind a
desire to waste the money for a boat ticket to Singapore which
Lepage had given to him, and to stay in Paris. Suddenly his ear
caught the conversation of the guests around him. He learned
of the Manchurian Incident, the first move of the Japanese
military to invade the Chinese continent. The French paper
that Kaneko borrowed from a garçon was filled with accusa-
tions against Japanese aggression. The matter was clearly ur-

gent. Kaneko immediately wrote to Michiyo, advising her to return to Japan as soon as she could, and he took a train for Marseilles that night.

The Japanese ship Kaneko boarded at Marseilles provided him with more news: it was feared that the military actions in Manchuria would spread to Shanghai and throughout China; and Japanese business was terribly afraid of losing raw materials in Southeast Asia. Through a student in the same cabin, Kaneko also learned that the proletarian writers who had once exerted strong influence on the Japanese public had been completely suppressed and that literature was still under the strict government censorship. However, the colonies and ports where the ship stopped looked peaceful under the flags of Britain, Holland, and France, exhibiting no signs of trouble. The colonialists' houses were peaceful and their spacious gardens were beautifully maintained. The Hindu and Tamil coolies, too, looked undisturbed, forever working slowly at construction sites and piers in India and Singapore.

In Singapore, Kaneko was surprised by the fact that Saijō Yaso (1892-1970), a writer of many popular juvenile songs as well as romantic poems, and a professor of French at Waseda University, had a strong influence on the personnel of the Japanese-language newspapers. He was informed that Japanese journalists in Singapore were split in factions and that one of them was financially bound to Saijō. It was a revelation for Kaneko to discover how the invisible capitalists operated in the South Seas and how a Japanese man of letters could exert his power far away from home. Kaneko wondered if Japan was a country worth returning to. At any rate, he had to raise money in order to repay Lepage and possibly to buy a ticket to Japan for himself.

Kaneko again entered the back country of the Malay Peninsula. In the burning sky of the tropics white clouds were churning as if they were sucking up all the phenomena below, and in the corner of the sky darkness was quickly spreading. A mysterious half-breed woman who spoke broken Japanese on the street of Batu Pahat made Kaneko realize how lonely he was. He had heard about the Japanese who "evaporated" in the jungle of Malaysia. It seemed easy for him to completely sever himself from Michiyo, Ken, Japan, and all else and to walk into the jungle, never to return. At that time a kind

Japanese man gave him a warning: the half-breed beauty was a
divorcée, daughter of an entrepreneur who was tied to the underworld of Batu Pahat. The Japanese in the rubber plantations were the same as before, hungry for visitors, and appreciated Kaneko's outdated "news" of Japan and his portrait
sketches.

Gradually, poetry returned to Kaneko. He jotted down
poems in a sketch book. As he wrote, his pen flowed and images sprang afresh. One poem in which he treated sharks grew
to be a long work. As the poems increased in quantity, he was
able to laugh at the news that he obtained when he got back to
Singapore. An attaché of the Japanese embassy told him that a
newspaper in Japan scornfully reported that Kaneko was seen
working as a drummer at an Indian port. It was partly pleasing
and partly frightening to learn that some people in Japan still
remembered him. Kaneko tried to picture in his mind the state
of the Japanese literary world, but it was far away and vague,
and he had no idea whether he could cope with it if he returned. In a small room of a transit hotel called Sakura, he
stealthily polished his poems.

Meanwhile, Kaneko noticed that the attitudes of the
Chinese toward him changed. The aggressive action of the
Japanese military in Manchuria was apparently continuing,
aggravating the Chinese in the South. Kaneko witnessed
Japanese being refused entrance to Chinese stores or rides in
rickshaws. It was perhaps time for Kaneko to leave Singapore.
Then suddenly, one day in April 1932, the manager of the
Sakura Hotel rushed to tell Kaneko that he had found Michiyo
on board a ship just arrived in the port. Michiyo had managed
to conclude her stay in Antwerp and was returning to Japan.
Swinging a red parasol Michiyo came to the Sakura Hotel. Her
report that she ate in the second-class dining room with a male
passenger, despite her third-class cabin ticket, needed no
additional explanation to Kaneko. Michiyo had acquired a new
lover whom she had met on the boat. Kaneko confronted the
lover a few hours before the boat departed. One of the many
painters who lived in Paris, Michiyo's lover insisted that he
would make Michiyo happy. Kaneko simply told Michiyo to
inform her parents that he would some day return to Japan and
he would raise Ken.

Two months passed. Kaneko was helped by a journalist

named Matsubara in Java, who offered to lend him 500 yen. Just after Kaneko purchased a boat ticket to Japan, he heard from Michiyo that Ken was sick and that he was needed in Japan.

CHAPTER 3

"A Seal": 1933-1945

M ANY things had changed in Japan. Michiyo's parents had
moved from Nagasaki to Ujiyamada, near Nagoya. Ken,
now seven years old, had recovered from his illness. Michiyo
had left Ken again and was apparently active in writers' circles
in Tokyo. Some of Kaneko's acquaintances had sunk into
obscurity. Titles of magazines and names of writers were
mostly unfamiliar to him. Kaneko felt as if he were a foreigner,
even though all faces he saw around him were unmistakably
Japanese.

Indeed, rarely had there been a busier period for the world
of Japanese poetry in terms of output and activity than that
time. As poets outgrew the state of *shintaishi* and began writing their works in the modern colloquial language, they were
confronted with Symbolism, Dadaism, anarchism, and other
trends and techniques imported from abroad. They hastily di-
gested them, wading through new translations from Western
literature. They formed, disbanded, and reorganized groups
and societies, while launching, discontinuing, and republish-
ing poetry journals. Only a handful of them were significant,
however. Takahashi Shinkichi (1901-   ), who in 1923 shocked
the world of letters with the totally unconventional style and
content of *Dadaist Shinkichi's Poems (Dadaist Shinkichi no
shi)*, exerted his influence for a long time. Trying to move
away from Takahashi, some poets inclined toward anarchism,
and they launched their journal called *The Red and the Black
(Aka to kuro)*. Because of its argumentative character, this
group was nicknamed as "terrorists in the poetic world" and
was annoyed by critics. One member of this group, Hagiwara
Kyōjirō (1899-1938), who had published his collection of
poems called *The Death Sentence (Shikei senkoku)* in 1925,

was particularly noted for his vehement accusation of social vice which he made through his poems. Their outcry was supported by such poets as Okamoto and Ono Tōzaburō (1903-   ), who rejected established political, social, and literary institutions and concepts. Compared with the Dadaist or the anarchist views, the so-called "Democratic School," which centered around Kaneko's old friends Momota and Tomita, was moderate in thought and expression. But they too were concerned with social issues and tried to reach out to the public by composing rather unsophisticated narrative poems. Momota began editing a journal called *An Acorn (Shii no mi)* in 1926, while Tomita remained devoted to Edward Carpenter. On the other hand, lyricists, led by Hagiwara, were equally active. Many lyricists, including Saijō, admired Hagiwara as "a creator of modern poetry in colloquial style." They contributed their works to the *Donkey (Roba)*, a journal started in 1926 by Hagiwara's old friend Muroo Saisei (1889-1962). The poets' zeal had spread to Japan's overseas territory and concessions, too. In Port Arthur Kitagawa Fuyuhiko (1900-   ) and Anzai Fuyue (1898-1965) launched *Asia (A)* in 1924, and exerted considerable influence on poetry in Japan. They rejected long poems and trimmed their works to an almost unintelligible minimum. Kaneko and Michiyo's friend Kusano, who used splendid onomatopoeia to hide his sharp social criticism, also launched in 1925 a Japanese journal called the *Drum (Dora)* in Canton, China.

In 1926 Nakano Shigeharu (1902-   ), a noted poet of the Proletarian School, classified contemporary poets into three categories: "Fantasts," "Nostalgists," and "Noisemakers."[1] "Fantasts" meant the Dadaists and importers of surrealistic techniques; "Nostalgists" included lyricists and classicists; and "Noisemakers" denoted proletarian and anarchist writers, those who shouted their political slogans in their works. Of these, the "Noisemakers" seemed most confused, as if lacking direction, though Nakano himself, evidently one of them, was really a more reserved poet who depended much on his artistic techniques and lyricism. Their confusion was due partly to government censorship, but more to internal problems. In 1926 the Japan Proletarian Literary Art League (*Nihon Puroretaria Bungei Remmei*), a national society for leftists, became nonfunctional and was reorganized as the Japan Proletarian Art League (*Nihon Puroretaria Geijutsu Remmei*). However, the new league also developed internal disputes, and in 1928 it reorganized itself as the All Japan Proletarian Art League (*Zen Nihon Musansha Geijutsu Remmei*). This league launched the *Battle Flag* (*Senki*), the journal which published Communist Kobayashi Takiji's (1903-1933) famous novel *The Factory Ship* (*Kanikōsen*), and other novels and essays. Concurrently, there was another group, the Workers and Farmers Art League (*Rō-Nō Geijutsuka Remmei*), which published a journal called the *Literary Battle Front* (*Bungei sensen*). Added to these, there was the Society of Proletarian Poets (*Puroretaria Shijin Kai*), which published the journal *Proletarian Poetry* (*Puroretaria shi*). On top of all these publications, anthologies were frequently compiled on a bipartisan basis, as if to balance the powers of these different groups.

On the other hand, many nonpolitical poets supported the journal *Poetry and Poetics* (*Shi to shiron*), which maintained a kind of art-for-art's-sake attitude. The editor of *Poetry and Poetics*, Haruyama Yukio (1902-   ), classified contemporary poets into four groups, namely, Decadents, Sentimentalists, Democrats, and Realists, and expressed his opposition to all on the grounds that none of them possessed any concrete poetics. According to Nishiwaki Junzaburō (1894-   ), a key contributor to *Poetry and Poetics*, the poet must feel and express the fundamental meaninglessness of reality, and to do so he must ignore the conventional usage of objects by juxtaposing them in his poetry as far apart in time and space as possible. The actual poems in *Poetry and Poetics* were best described as impressionistic, containing novel expressions and layers of imagery which were in no progressive order. To many they looked like a complicated mosaic of contrasting words and imageries. Some poems were as short as the seventeen-syllable *haiku*, which utilized a sharp contrast of imagery in its small form. The poets in *Poetry and Poetics* called such works *poésies* in French and distinguished them from *gendaishi*, or modern Japanese poetry, which they did not favor. They also upheld a slogan, "l'esprit nouveau," and claimed that they were a part of the literary movement developed by modernists in Europe and America.

Poetry and Poetics, too, developed internal disputes, and in 1930 some members walked out to launch a new journal. The group in dissent included Kitagawa and Miyoshi Tatsuji (1900-1964), and their new journal was *Poetry: Reality* (*Shi genjutsu*). Concerned about balancing artistic problems with political and social issues, *Poetry: Reality* published works of both lyricists like Hagiwara and leftists like Kubokawa Tsuruj-irō (1903-   ). Meanwhile, the energetic Kitagawa began editing another journal, *Time* (*Jikan*), in April 1931.

Behind these movements, there was the dark shadow of growing militarism in the country. Censorship became more severe than ever before. Particularly after the Manchurian Incident the government's control over literature was enormously intensified. Offices of the organizations were searched for illegal papers, groups were ordered to disband, and some individuals were put under surveillance. Active Communist writers, such as Nakano and Kubokawa, were arrested. In the corners of the ravaged world of letters were faint voices of lament. A few advocated that poetry should be free from politics and called for a literary "renaissance."

In the summer of 1932 Kaneko rented a small room on the second floor of Takedaya Inn in Shinjuku, Tokyo. He had virtually nothing to furnish it with. When he was hungry, he visited Michiyo, who lived in a nearby apartment. Often he found Michiyo, surrounded by her friends and magazine editors, talking about French literature and the beauty of the Seine. She was apparently a rising star, whom Kaneko watched with awe. It was at least a relief for Kaneko that Michiyo seemed to have completely forgotten about the young man with whom, before they went to Europe, she had had an affair. Kaneko would go back to Takedaya Inn and read and reread the manuscripts he had brought back from Singapore. The room was noisy. On the streets of Tokyo there were always a lot of people, day or night. The crowd, composed only of the Japanese, seemed to Kaneko to be moving in one direction, as indicated in the following poem, "A Seal" ("*Ottosei*"):

A Seal

1

Smelly breath,
Steaming.

Slimy skin, like a tomb.

It makes me sick,
What a disgusting life!

Bodies—
Ponderous air-filled bags.

Sluggish resilience.
Pitiful rubber.
How conceited!
Mediocre!

Pock marks mar their skin:
Huge balls.

Pushed aside by the fishy nauseating crowd,
I have always longed for the opposite direction.

To me,
The cities they mobbed and occupied
Were as desolate as the Alaska
I had seen in an old film.

2

The crowd, called people!
It was they who expelled Voltaire and imprisoned Grotius:
The same creatures polluting the earth, from Batavia to Lisbon, with
    gossip and dust.
Those who sneeze and spit through their whiskers; those with
    prudish airs and stifling yawns; those noisy groups pointing fingers
    at and accusing any one who deviates from conventions, labeling
    him a traitor or madman. They intermarry to maintain this trait.
    They are of the same blood; they belong to the same clique. Their
    innumerable ties and the resulting wall of bodies block even the
    ocean current.
The light of the Arctic sun fell on the hesitant water.
Along the horizon, where eyes cannot follow, a wire net was
    stretched.

Today is their wedding . . .
Yesterday, they had celebrations.
Somewhere, I hear an icebreaker operating.
Incessantly bowing, shaking fins, rolling bodies, they vied, soon
    clouding the sea with waste.

Fearing to leave the crowd that warmed their bodies, they begged for
    sympathy, crying in weak voices.

3

None of them noticed their iceberg, darker than midnight cities,
　crack and begin to drift.
Spreading their tails,
Some clumsily crept higher,
. . . talked even about literature.

Twilight scene!
A hanging scroll of the setting sun, frost-bitten and sore!

Among the crowd, worshipping unanimously, casting long shadows,
Is one
Who disdainfully faces the other way.
It is I.
I, who hate seals,
Yet, after all, I am only a seal.
But,
"A seal who faces the other way."[2]

This poem was not published until 1937, but it was among
the manuscripts that Kaneko worked on at Takedaya Inn. The
first line of the second stanza would be a revelation to the
reader, if he had failed to see the true nature of the seals in the
first stanza. Could there exist any other poetry so scathingly
critical of man as this? The masses called "the people" inter-
married, formed cliques, and held rites. In 1933, two leaders
of the Communist party issued statements from prison renouncing communism, and more than 500 political prisoners
followed suit within a month. Many people wrote about this
particular incident and about their own experiences in changing their "belief," so that a literary school called "Converted
Literature" (*tenkō bungaku*) was formed. Similarly, two leaders in the right wing formed a group called the Literary Con-
fabulation Society (*Bungei Konwa Kai*) and began publishing
a journal in January 1934. The society attracted famous writers
like Kawabata, Yokomitsu, and Shimazaki, among others, but it
soon disintegrated because of certain internal struggles, despite the strong backing it received from both the government
and financial superconglomerates like Mitsui and Mitsubishi.
Some indeed crept higher, as Kaneko wrote, and talked even
about literature.

Not many people came to visit Kaneko at Takedaya Inn.
Those who did were surprised at the sight of Kaneko's com-

pletely bare room. Kunikida came. He had spent all of the
royalties paid by the publishers for his father's novels, and he
was now an activist on the left. From Kunikida, Kaneko
learned of the reality of the leftist movement. There was news
that the Communist novelist Kobayashi, who authored *The
Factory Ship*, was tortured to death only several hours after he
was arrested by the secret police. Also through Kunikida,
Kaneko became acquainted with Nakano. A poet and critic,
Nakano read Kaneko's manuscripts and was impressed by the
strength of the theme and the techniques employed to present
the theme. He promised Kaneko to help publish them, but he
found it difficult at that time to locate a publisher willing to
print poems that might be mistaken as Communist. While
waiting for the poems to be published, Kaneko had to make a
living and, above all, to remedy his relationship with Michiyo.
He had to write more, too, if he were to continue living.

It was Kaneko's real mother, Ōshika Ryō, who helped
Kaneko this time. Ryō informed Kaneko of her daughter Sute's
plan to establish a cosmetics manufacturing company and advised him to serve as advertising consultant. She also made
arrangements so that Kaneko, Michiyo, and Ken could live together. Kaneko was placed on the payroll of his sister's company at a salary of fifty yen a month. For the first time in his
life, Kaneko had a steady income and lived in a house with his
wife and son, although Michiyo maintained a separate apartment as an "office" for her work. Kaneko was responsible for
coining the company name, Moncoco, and other French-
sounding names for its products. He also drew pictures to decorate the wrappers of the products. Ryō was pleased to see
Kaneko settled down, for both Kaneko's real father and elder
brother had committed some crime and the family had been in
a sorry condition. The father died in 1935 in distress, and Ryō,
too, died in the same year.

Kaneko wished to publish the manuscripts that he had
brought back from Singapore as a book. But as a prerequisite
to publishing a book, he had to become better known in the
journalistic world. Besides, he himself felt uneasy, not knowing the present literary currents well, and some catch-up work
seemed in order. As his life was somewhat stabilized, he read
many works by contemporary poets and gradually began publishing his writings, mostly essays, in *Japanese Poetry* (*Nihon
shi*) and other little magazines. Finally, in September 1935,

the *Literary Arts* (*Bungei*) published a piece from the manuscripts. This was "The Sharks" ("*Samé*"). In this renowned
work, the sharks are first described in the same way as "the
seals," but of course they are more cunning and more powerful:

Their skin, clammy
Sickening and smelly.

Hauled on deck,
They resemble ceramic tubs;
With neither heads
Nor tails.
In the water they are huge; vicious cannons, dark ominous nuzzles.
Dividing the world like Moses' miracle, they appear and disappear
    like scythes of death.

The sharks;
Swords
Dangerous, just sharpened;
Irritation glittering like a blade.
The cruel
Heartless clique, rampant in the world.[3]

"The Sharks" consists of 297 lines in six sections. It is a powerful poem, compared with most contemporary poetry. What is
truly impressive, however, is the internal structure, rather
than the external, and the superb techniques bracing it. There
is, in this poem, a whole history of conflicts between East and
West, as viewed against the scenery of Southeast Asia through
the poet's critical eye. There is also a bitter, relentless, but
solid self flashing in the beguiling imagery and brilliant diction. While the sharks in the poem could be mere animals at
sea, they are also war-headed torpedoes, domineering colonialists, or anything that the poet wishes. And the poet is a
wanderer, who, earlier in "The Song of Wandering," had
dreamed of a merry picnic scene dotted with Spanish umbrellas.

I wander with a black umbrella,
Feeling giddy in the water.
For five, seven, ten years,
Alas, my fingers eaten, my body half-devoured,
I have been tossed, hindered by a strong current,
On the equator, in Sumatra Strait.

The world sneered at me, but I didn't take it seriously.
A stupid life, mine; a vicious circle!
My guts hurt, so completely washed.
Still, blood oozes;
The sharks rush at me.
Hiding my terror, I salute them like Chaplin.
But the sharks only pass by,
Moving my body slightly.

Why don't they eat me?
Because of the venom in my heart?
Is my body tasteless or rotten?
Occasionally some take a bite, but they spit me out.
Taunting, triumphant,
They take time for digestion.
Dare they be epicureans?[4]

"The Sharks" is not, as commonly defined, "a poem of resistance." Nor is it merely an impeachment of the imperialists. Roaming Southeast Asian countries, Kaneko searches for his Self. He writes in Sections Four and Five:

4

Where has it come from—this wayward wave?
Emden?
No, it could not have;
This floating mine,
Passing through the Strait of Malacca where ripples are like fireflies.
A shark's nose skims it.
Knowing it is explosive,
Elated, he chuckles.
He has a scar on his cheek
Like Singapore's governor Clifford,
Who resembled Hitler.

His haughty, broad, rough, cruel, whetstone profile utters,
"You aren't even a citizen, let alone a loyalist.
You vagabond, beggar, rogue, outcast."

I, having a wife and son,
Could not reply;
Wife's legs shredded and son's hips eaten;
Threads of flesh floating.

I gathered my strength to attack,

They were a wall, a barricade called "society."
It was raining;
Ripples on the sea—a lonely promenade.
I drifted away,
Hoping to meet another mine.

5

Now I wander in dark woods of the sea, in the dimly-lit rusty water,
    through Bintan Canal, in Makasar Bay, on the equator, outside the
    port of Sunda.
A river slit a jungle's throat. Black plague.
The Pahang, the Batang Kali, and the Perak irrigate palms and wash
    mud into the sea.
Dead trees being burned.
Caramel-colored paddies.
Mosquitoes hatching. A customs office.
The ports of Telok Anson, Kolaka, and Palembang.

Rotten rubber melting like tar.

Not edible, nor smokable like opium.
The Moslem, eyes sunken,
Crouches motionlessly on a long pier.
I pass these ports.
The sun scorches filth, death, my skull.
Leeches and maggots around the latrines, writhing.
A blue heron perched on a lofty tree.

Narrow belt-like scene about to sink with the tide.
The water surface glares like a reflector.
The sharks have followed me even here.
I see their ceramic bellies.
Cutting muddy water,
Razor-like calcium flashes.

The sharks, persistent;
They never miss.
Never scared away
Coolly they run me down.

The coral reef, Lat. 8°S., Long. 115°E.
A tortoise in the red flowers.
Anemones like a mantle.
On the waves, a colorful peacock,
Dazed as if

I had fine peppermint—actually bad alcohol.
Bitter salt water; a Borneo boat, tossed like a butterfly.

From Timor to New Guinea,
The sea was like a maiden forest,
I was lonely, as if in a rich man's salon.

The sea—this beguiling confusion,
And those who spoil it, the makers of the abyss, the sharks.
They hunt me down
With their rhombic snouts.

Unanimously they shout,
"Humanity, peace, love."
They from a clique; their law, public opinion, concepts;
A sure way to disintegrate man.[5]

    The majority of critics and poets did not recognize the author of "The Sharks." Apparently, subscribers to the *Literary Arts* did not bother to read this long poem. Some of those who read it thought that there appeared a bold young poet who was unfamiliar with the trend in the poetic world. A few, however, saw the uniqueness and power in "The Sharks." To those few, the short, unintelligible poems, sentimental musical poems, shouting political poems, and other contemporary poems seemed suddenly insignificant. They were struck by Kaneko's vision; his creative nihilism that encompassed the past and the present, the Occidental and the Japanese; and his superb techniques which, unlike those of other Japanese poets, sustained the power of the long poem. For Kaneko, poetry was fundamentally a probing into his own soul. On this point he shared Hagiwara's sensitivity. Kaneko thrust his probing needle like a weapon into the object that threatened his existence, whereas Hagiwara quivered at his nervous probing into his own neurotic soul and trembled at the threat from the world outside him. The sixth and final part of "The Sharks" reads:

Alas, I, corpse among corpses, still a youthful body wandering in adversity, my soul!
Despising conventions and factionalism, avoiding personal ties, I will not be satisfied if I destroy the earth seven times over.
Outside of the world that hates me, blames, and scorns me,
I, pretending indifference,
Wallow in the sea, gulping the salty water.

How severe, the torture of heat on merciless water!
Exhausted with wandering from east to south, south to southwest,
    amid the spit, urine, and melon seeds,
Alas, why do I continue wandering?

My wife clinging to my arm,
My son hanging on my neck,
I have no choice but to fight back,
I need strength, but there's no time for hesitation; no way to scheme,
    nor to flatter; completely deprived and seriously wounded,
I bare my chest to lure their attack.

The sharks,
Shrewdly, do not move,
Staring at us through narrowed eyes,
Greedy though they are, they are too full to attack.
Stomachs filled with undigested humans,
One by one they turn their backs!

Their bodies are rusted;
Some like broken chimneys,
Dented or bent
Their sides,
Riddled with bullet holes,
Smelling of new paint.
The sharks.
The sharks.
The sharks.
Curse them.
Destroy them.[6]

Shortly after "The Sharks" appeared in the *Literary Arts*,
Kaneko had a visitor, who gave his name as Hatanaka Shigeo.
Hatanaka was an editor of the prestigious magazine the *Public
Review* (*Chūō kōron*), and he urged Kaneko to contribute
poems like "The Sharks" to the *Public Review*. This was the
beginning of the long, trustful relationship between Kaneko
and the Chūō Kōron Publishing Co., which was to publish
many other works by Kaneko, as well as his complete works
posthumously. Kaneko began receiving decent royalties for
his manuscripts.

In 1936 Kaneko was forty years old. The Moncoco Company
was doing well, and Kaneko was financially secure. He moved
to a larger house in the same block. Michiyo was also doing

well as a novelist; she was a principal member of the group which published a journal called *Literary Writings* (*Bungaku sōshi*). Ken seemed to be enjoying the new house and school, too. At this jovial time, Kaneko helped his foster mother, Sumi, to remarry, serving as matchmaker between Sumi and Tominaga Kenji. Tominaga was the father of Tominaga Tarō (1901-1925), a shortlived poet, and Tominaga Jirō (1909-1969), a novelist who wrote for *Literary Writings*. Kaneko became a stepbrother of the Tominaga brothers and was happy. He even had leisure time to appreciate a large pomegranate tree in the yard of his house.

But on February 26, 1936, "a most shocking event" occurred. Young army officers staged a coup d'etat and occupied the central district of Tokyo, killing and wounding important government officials. The entire city was immediately placed under curfew and it was ominously quiet. Kaneko wanted to know more about the situation when Kunikida came. Now an activist of the left, Kunikida was upset, his face pale. He hurriedly asked Kaneko to help him hide certain materials somewhere in Kaneko's house. They dug a hole in the yard near the pomegranate tree and buried materials that individuals were prohibited to read.[7] There was snow on the ground. Darkened at heart by the news of the victorious military, Kaneko walked in the city, unable to suppress his irritation, disappointment, and anger. This was the same incident that later "shocked" the novelist Mishima Yukio (1925-1970) and caused him to write fanatic novels and dramas and to produce a macabre movie, all in spiritual support of the action of the military. Kaneko wrote:

I came to realize that all reforms had been like this and warned myself to be more cautious from now on, particularly if it concerned ideological and political reforms. I once cherished liberalism; now I became reluctant to declare my stand. I decided to pretend, among other possibilities, to be an idler. I am not coward; I am only trying to remain fair and just.[8]

In August 1937 "The Sharks" was published along with six other poems in book form by Jimmin Bunko (People's Library) Publisher. The book, *The Sharks* (*Samé*), had on its cover a large Chinese character meaning "shark" decoratively written by Yü Ta-fu, the Chinese liberal whom Kaneko had met in Shanghai in 1928. Kaneko had kept the calligraphy since the previous year, when Yü secretly came to Japan to contact Kuo Mo-jo, who had been in Japan as a political exile. It was ironical that, when the book was being printed, the war between Japan and China started. Only about fifty copies of *The Sharks* were sold.[9]

From the end of that year to January 1938, Kaneko and Michiyo were in China, where the war was already going on. The "official" purpose of their trip was to study the Chinese market for some laundry products of Moncoco. They had to submit complicated forms to the authorities, but, encouraged by Hatanaka of the *Public Review*, they figured it worthwhile. Kaneko expected that the trip would enable him to determine "the way to discount the news (about the war in newspapers and magazines.)"[10] As expected, Kaneko saw with his own eyes many "Merchants of Death" operating in China. In Tientsin he saw even cabarets and bars run by businessmen from Osaka, as well as branches of Japanese department stores. There Kaneko met a civilian, Hayasaka Jirō, who openly criticized the big business firm, Mitsui, for its shrewd acquisition of the exclusive rights to retrieve cannon shells on the war front. He heard later that Hayasaka was killed by the military police.[11]

On New Year's Day of 1938 Kaneko was at the Great Wall near Peking. The area on the way had had a flood and was frozen. It was a peculiar scene. Kaneko was told that under the solid ice there was a village where Japanese soldiers had killed Chinese farmers and raped women.

I knew the long history of the British exploitation in India and of the forced labor by the Dutch in Java, so I had not accepted at face value the "righteousness" of the Western countries. Similarly, I did not think that the "righteousness" of Japan should be accepted as far as the war against China was concerned. War is militarists' trade. For them, to be righteous means to be winning. However, I felt that in this particular war the ambition of the Japanese public took part even more than that of the militarists. I sensed it in the crowds of people on the streets in Tōkyo. Was it not that the fascists in Japan had taken advantage of the public's ambition? It must be that the Japanese, deadlocked in decadence, earnestly hoped for the military to break them out of the deadlock and to open a new road for their survival. As if to prove this theory, the people whom I met, whether intellectuals or not, would argue for the war, trying to convince me that the war was something divine and absolute.[12]

It was hard for Kaneko to believe that the Japanese, who, not long ago, had violently protested to the government against only a one-*sen* increase in the public transportation fare, were now so unanimously going along with the military. There were, however, a small number of people who shared Kaneko's feelings. They were the editors of the *Public Review* and the Jimmin Bunko Publisher, which continued to publish Kaneko's poems. One of these poems was "My Parachute" ("*Rakkasan*"), published in the June 1938 issue of the *Public Review*. In the second stanza of "My Parachute," the poet, clinging helplessly to a falling parachute, asked what was under his feet. It was his country. But the words of the poet, who decided to be "reluctant to declare my stand," must not be taken at face value.

> I'm lucky, born there
> Country of "Victory"
> Where women have been chaste
> Since grandfather's time.
>
> Jests and fish-bones,
> Smiles of hunger,
> Strict discipline,
> Shabby clothes—
> The pitiful scene.
>
> My countrymen live there
> Narrow brows, sharp eyes, bony shoulders,
> Fellow countrymen
> Who not only speak Japanese
> But read my face.
>
> "Warriors
> Drink
> On trust."
>
> Electric poles stuck in the flood.
> National flags
> Sway on thatched roofs.
> Scattered cherry petals, honor of dying:
> The newly erected monument
> For the war dead; homes
> Bound by convention;
> Miniature garden
> And Fuji-shaped ornament.

3

Still falling I close my eyes
Rub my soles together
Pray:
"Please, God,
Land me safely in my country,
Do not blow me out to the sea,
Let not my homeland vanish
Like a dream beneath my feet."
I pray
That I may not be repelled
By earth's gravity
And reach nowhere,
Falling, falling, and falling.[13]

The scenery under his feet was none other than his native land. He could see it better than he did when he roamed Southeast Asia and Europe—better perhaps than Takamura Kōtarō (1883-1956) did in Paris when he wrote the famous poem called "The Land of *Netsuke*" ("*Netsuke no kuni*").[14] Like Takamura, Kaneko regarded the Japanese as being narrow-browed, sharp-eyed, and bony-shouldered, completely satisfied with frugality, chastity, and strict discipline, like the *netsuke*, or miniature sculpture, they cherished. From the helplessly drifting parachute, the poet viewed Japan as a flooded miniature garden where houses with Japanese flags and some war memorials were sticking out of water.

Kaneko was different from Takamura, who once despised the Japanese and later tumbled into thinking that the Japanese race was divine, but in danger from British and American invasion. Kaneko prayed that he might not be repelled by earth's gravity, that he might land safely in his native land. Floating in the sky, with nobody around, Kaneko knew that he must not land in the sea. As always, he was aware that he was one of the masses he loathed, and his loathing was backed by his love for mankind of which he was one. "My Parachute" perfectly balanced cynicism and truth, revolt and attachment, buoyancy and gravity, and hatred and love under an obvious yet beguiling veil.

Hatanaka, who had published "My Parachute" in *The Public Review*, was later imprisoned and not released until after the end of World War II. Kaneko continued to publish, whenever he found the opportunity to do so. As for Michiyo, she was a popular novelist, commercially more successful than Kaneko, and was sought after by publishers. The cosmetics company prospered, managed by an able business man who was also a publisher of a popular ladies' journal. Kaneko and Michiyo bought a better house in Kichijōji, at that time on the outskirts of Tokyo, and moved there.

There were virtually no pronounced leftist writers remaining in the Japanese world of letters. Those who refused to change their belief were in prison. Many had confessed their "conversion" to support the rightists. Some quietly withdrew from writing, while the others continued to act as tools of the authorities. The majority of the poets belonged to either one of two factions: Shiki (Four Seasons) or Rekitei (Historical Course). *Shiki* was the title of a journal, launched in 1933, and *Rekitei* was a journal begun in 1935. Except that the former group admired Hagiwara as its mentor and the latter's leader was Takamura, the two were not fundamentally different: they both were nonpolitical, basically lyricist, and both were concerned with the perfection of techniques. Kaneko contributed a few works to the *Historical Course (Rekitei)* when his friend Kusano edited it. The rest of the time he remained alone. Quite understandably, he did not like to be with the masses. To join a clique to him meant to abandon his Self.

The "incident" in China seemed never to end. The war dragged on and it appeared to be escalating to a major international conflict. The National Mobilization Act came into force and all Japanese, whether military or civilian, were expected to carry out work in support of the military effort. The draft age was lowered and, on the international scene, the Triple Alliance was formed among Germany, Italy, and Japan. In 1940, a year before the Pacific War broke out, Kaneko polished up his manuscript of the record of his roamings in Southeast Asia and published it as *The Journey through Malay and Dutch-India (Marei Ran-In kikō)*. Scarcely noticed by critics at the time, *The Journey through Malay and Dutch-India* was a curious contrast to the prevailing literature. The few who read it were disappointed when they did not find any description related to the war or to Japan's possible expansion to the south. No one noticed that *The Journey through Malay and Dutch-India* was a prose version of "The Sharks." There were palm trees in muddy water, a thicket of dark jungle, and torrential squalls; there were abandoned rubber plantations, Japanese clubhouses, and native laborers; and there were coolies and prostitutes subsisting at the lowest level of the tropical regions. But above all, there was the soul of a poet who, like the ancient Japanese poets, traveled alone in search of his place in the universe.

On December 8, 1941, Kaneko was in his house at Kichijōji. Radio stations stopped all regular programs and announced the outbreak of the Pacific War. Kaneko shouted one word, "Fools!" Michiyo and Ken were speechless, listening to the news of the Japanese attack on Pearl Harbor.

In April 1942, Tokyo was raided by American planes for the first time. In the following month about 3,100 writers, including scholars of Japanese literature, became members of the Japanese Literature Patriotic Society (*Nihon Bungaku Hōkoku Kai*). The Society was organized by a directive of the Cabinet Intelligence Bureau for the purpose of creating a leadership forum to generate a unified national opinion of the war, to heighten the spirit to fight, and to act in cooperation with the government's war efforts. The Society was also commissioned to formulate and propagate a nationalistic view of world literature through which to benefit writers and artists not only in Japan but in Asian countries. One of the honorary members was the old *shintaishi* poet and novelist Shimazaki. The Poetry Division of the Society was headed by two men: Saijō, whose name Kaneko had often heard in Singapore, and Takamura of *the Historical Course*. The members were busy preparing for the Conference of Writers in the Greater Asia. Co-prosperity Sphere to be held in 1943. The Society was planning to invite to this conference writers and artists from Asian countries that Japan then controlled, including China, Manchuria, Thailand, Malaysia, and Singapore, in order to transmit to them the glory and benefits of the Japanese empire.

Meanwhile, some writers were "drafted" and sent to the war front either as reporters or intelligence officers. Younger writers apparently considered this "draft" a better deal than the regular induction, and some of them were even willing to serve in such capacity. In 1942, Michiyo, too, was "drafted." Relieved to find out that the order came not from the army but from the Ministry of Foreign Affairs, Kaneko saw her plane shakily take off and head south. Michiyo returned safely by boat after having completed a lecture tour on the subject of Japanese classics. But Japan was not a safe place anymore. Kaneko had to build a bomb shelter in the yard and spent many sleepless nights in it. Takamura and Miyoshi's recent poems that expressed their views of the war as a sacred war seemed to Kaneko particularly meaningless. Satō Haruo disappointed Kaneko with his poems that praised the military actions. The titles of their poems, such as "National Exigency," "The Day of Crises," "The Imperial Proclamation of War," and "The Victory News," did not inspire Kaneko to read them. Kaneko was sad when he noticed his longtime friend Satō Sōnosuke, one of the few who had recognized Kaneko as a poet in the 1920s, publishing militaristic poems.

Some people were fortunate: they were excused, so to speak, from watching the decline of literature or the devastation of the country. Hagiwara, long a respected poet, died in May 1942. Soon Satō Sōnosuke passed away. Within the same year, the "Symbolist" Kitahara died. All these poets were still in their fifties. And in August 1943, the time when one of Japan's Triple Allies, Italy, was about to surrender, the illustrious *shintaishi* poet and novelist Shimazaki passed away at the age of seventy-two. Tokuda, whose novel *The Mould* had impressed Kaneko, died in the same year. Kaneko's foster mother, Sumi, who had come to live with Kaneko, became insane and, in the confusion of a heavy air raid, died.

Kaneko was healthy and in high spirits. He engaged in a discussion with some writers at one of the preparatory meetings for a proposed Conference of Writers in the Greater Asia Co-prosperity Sphere. He walked out of it after arguing unsuccessfully over the concept of the Greater Asia Co-prosperity Sphere. Only one other member, a specialist in Chinese literature, supported Kaneko's opinion that it would be meaningless to make the delegates from other Asian countries bow in front of the Imperial Palace. The last meeting he attended was to discuss the way to teach the Japanese language to the entire Malaysian population. He left the meeting totally disgusted, determined not to take part in any activity of the Japanese Literature Patriotic Society.

The fanatics flourished. They gave new interpretations to obscure historical events and literary records in Japan,

analogizing ordinary words and concepts to their own fancies.
Japan was said to be a country of eight islands abounding with
rice, according to an ancient Shinto prayer, and "eight islands"
were equated to "eight corners," a Chinese concept utilized
by a late-nineteenth-century Japanese nationalist to theorize
about his principle of the unification of all corners of the world
by the chrysanthemum-crested Japanese Imperial family.
Words seemed to exist only for the demagogue. Kaneko wrote,
as if to release his indignation:

A Bowl of Rice

A bowl of rice
Rises as days pass.

Just a bowl of rice
With lacquered chopsticks
Is as tall as snow-capped Fuji,
Japan's main food for generations.

You know, my friend,
I know too,
The warmth of rice
Filling our heart
Is our sorrow.

Salt of tears on rice
With sour plum, soaked in tea
Is meager food.

A frozen chrysanthemum,
Weak sun on a lattice-window,
And the patience of our women.

The rice steaming like a colored cloud,
This year, I trace the snowy path of Fuji;
Pray in secret:
May the bowl of rice not be hidden by the cloud
May war not spoil it, nor crumble it into pieces.[15]

Kaneko had evacuated Tokyo in 1943, with his well-to-do sister Sute's family, to a house by Lake Yamanaka near Mount
Fuji. He had hoped that the shortage of food, particularly of
rice, would be less severe in the countryside. But rice was
scarce. Other goods were also in short supply, and air-raid si-

rens sounded frequently. Almost every day Kaneko watched
B-29 bombers coming first toward Mount Fuji and then turning toward Tokyo. Long the beautiful symbol of Japan, Mount
Fuji was apparently used as a natural guidepost by the bombers. To the eye of Kaneko it was only too obvious that Tokyo
would be completely ruined and Japan would be defeated.

Kaneko's uncooperative attitude toward the war efforts
reached a pinnacle when he prevented Ken's military induction. It was a total waste, Kaneko thought, to allow his son to
be drafted. But in the beginning of 1945 a draft notice arrived.
Kaneko made the maximum use of Ken's mild illness in order
to disqualify him in the induction physical.[16] He confined Ken
in his study and, according to the now-legendary account,
burned raw pine needles to make Ken breathe the smoke in
order to cause an acute case of bronchitis. With further aid
from an old physician in the neighborhood, Dr. Nakayama
Shigeo, Ken escaped induction. Here is a poem, entitled "The
Lyric in Which Rev. Cotte Appears" ("*Kotto-san no detekuru
jojōshi*"), which Kaneko wrote at that time.

> Ken is watching
> Mom is watching
> The ice on the lake
> Immovable water
> Bubbles like beads
>
> Mom wants to skate
> Ken pretends
> To want to skate
> He is a sissy
>
> Beneath the ice
> Milky smoke
> Dark rings
> Like eyes of the dead
>
> Water contains
> Its own weight
> Only spring
> Would break it out
>
> "War is a chronic illness
> After this will be spring"
> Rev. Cotte says

Let us believe him, Ken
But honestly this winter
Is too long for Mom and Dad

You enjoy spring
We don't care
The precious time of ours
Wasted in the storm

Rev. Cotte lies
Sick in bed
"No food
No fuel"

What there is in this world
Is only despair
. . .[17]

By the lake near Mount Fuji, Kaneko and Michiyo were the closest in their life. They had saved Ken. Spring was supposed to follow winter, but the winter in the final year of the war was particularly harsh and long. Rev. Joseph Cotte (1875-1949) was the Director of the Athénée Français in Tokyo. The shortage of food and fuel was hard on this old Frenchman and Rev. Cotte became ill. Kaneko took care of him and, persuading the villagers, who were prejudiced against any Caucasian, put him in a hospital in a nearby town.[18]

On one of those days in 1945, the "anarchist" Okamoto visited Kaneko. They were friends of long standing: back in 1928 Kaneko had demonstrated to Okamoto his skill in drawing erotic pictures, and in 1940, Kaneko, Okamoto, and a few other poets, including Tsuboi, had managed a poetry journal called the *Poetic Source* (*Shigen*). They shared another memory, an incident in which Kaneko had saved Okamoto's life. Okamoto, a little drunk, had angered an army officer in a restaurant in Tokyo. Opposing military personnel during the war was suicide for civilians. The officer was about to draw his sword to kill Okamoto, but Kaneko managed to smooth over the situation. Now, in the isolated village near Mount Fuji, Kaneko and Okamoto gave vent to their resentment against the military. They talked about censorship, publishing houses relinquished after air raids, cessation of magazines, lack of

paper, rationed food and daily needs, and deaths of their acquaintances. Yet their resentment was never stilled.

Kaneko showed Okamoto a draft of his recent poems, telling
him that it became so cold by Mount Fuji that often he had to
thaw the ink to write them. Okamoto was deeply impressed by
Kaneko's story, his unyielding spirit, and his poems. This, incidentally, motivated Okamoto to launch, immediately after
the end of the war, a journal called *The Cosmos* (*Kosumosu*) in
his hope to publish these wartime poems by Kaneko.
Okamoto, too, had perhaps foreseen Japan's defeat. However,
Kaneko was to put out the poems not in Okamoto's journal, but
in book form—in fact, in four books: *My Parachute* (*Rakkasan*)
and *The Moth* (*Ga*) in 1948, and *An Elegy for Women* (*Onna-
tachi e no erejii*) and *The Song of the Devil's Son* (*Oni no ko no
uta*) in 1949.

As the Japanese naval power was destroyed, the army
perished on the islands in the Pacific. Iwo Jima and Saipan
literally changed their shape as a result of the enormous bom-
bardment. The air raids over Japan became more severe than
before, and cities burned day and night. Japanese who had
been indoctrinated to the national slogan *"Ichioku isshin"*
(One hundred million Japanese serve the country as one)
began seriously talking instead about *"Ichioku gyokusai"*
(One hundred million deaths and no surrender). Kaneko, "a
seal who faces the other way," wished this slogan be changed
to "Ninety-nine million nine hundred ninety-nine thousand
nine hundred ninety-nine Japanese serve the country as one."
Actually, the majority of young and middle-aged Japanese men
were out of the country, if they were alive, and there were
much fewer than 100 million people in the land. Soon the
Japanese allies in Europe surrendered, and material supplies
in Japan dwindled to nothing. Japan's last battleship Yamato
sank, and Okinawa fell. Women, children, and the elderly produced bamboo spears as their only weapons against atom
bombs and armored landing crafts, and they awaited the zero
hour. Japan's defeat was imminent.

CHAPTER 4

The Tragedy of Man: *1946-1956*

In the Ruins

A moon
scatters in the ashes and bones—
a plate on a juggler's stick.

In these ruins
I sift the light,
panning gold.

Has love died
or sorrow?
There is the smell of death—
smoking bodies
twisted loins,
and the tarnished silence
cuts at my heart.

White mushroom,
your misty stage
is deserted.

A dark line of a river
flows
in the milky expanse.[1]

THE Pacific War was over. But another war had started. Those who escaped death had to confront the devastation of the country and fight for their own survival. People were tired. Nearly everyone had lost someone close to him. Those who were lucky awaited the return of a loved one from the war front. From Manchuria, Korea, China, and other former ter-

ritories of Japan, weary civilians returned. From Southeast
Asia and the Pacific islands disarmed soldiers began to be sent
back. Cities had been destroyed. Farmlands were wasted. All
commodities were extremely scarce. Food was particularly
hard to acquire. The currency was frozen, and new monetary
notes with far less value than the old money were issued. And
the country was under the strict control of foreign forces for
the first time in its long history. People's morale was low.

Kaneko's house in Tokyo had escaped being bombed, but
Kaneko was so accustomed to living in a village near Mount
Fuji that he was afraid of returning to ruined Tokyo. Besides,
his house was occupied by four families who refused to move
out. A lot of people had no place to go. There were many or-
phans. And every railway station was filled with such people.
One day at Kichijōji Station, near his house, Kaneko saw his
old-time friend Yokomitsu. He was struck by the impoverished
figure of Yokomitsu, at one time the leader of the School of
New Feeling. Looking lean and tired, Yokomitsu retained
nothing to suggest his past glory, often compared to that of
Kawabata, who, unlike Yokomitsu, lived to receive a Nobel
Prize. Kaneko and Yokomitsu talked and laughed, admitting
that they had both become like hermits. A few minutes later, a
train came and they parted. They never saw each other again.
Kaneko recalled Yokomitsu's kindness in the past, which had
enabled him to make some money when he was impoverished. He also remembered Yokomitsu's novel *Shanghai*, which reminded him of his days in Shanghai and his unsuccessful attempt at winning a prize by writing a novel.
Kaneko found lice in the seams of his clothes, as always, after
he returned from Tokyo to the village on a crowded train.

Fortunately, Moncoco Cosmetics still had some raw materials, which it could sell at unbelievably inflated prices. It was
the enterprising women, Sute and Michiyo, who got the family's economy going in crisis. Black markets had sprung up in
the ruins; there were no stores as such. Everything from dum-
plings to used clothing and shoes was sold or bartered in the
open from hand to hand. Kaneko sometimes witnessed people
stealing large cans of vaseline from the storage of Moncoco
Cosmetics and carrying them away in broad daylight. Many
were desperate. The poorest were usually the ex-soldiers who
had just returned from the war front. The biggest spenders in

the marketplace were those who supplied the basic needs: farmers or the producers of rice, and "pom-pom girls," or the Japanese prostitutes, so nicknamed by the soldiers of the Allied Occupation Forces. Because of the land reform enforced by the Occupation authorities, the farm workers, who had been dominated for centuries by the landlords, became the owners of land. Many farming families, spared by the air raids during the war, were better off, but the majority of the Japanese were miserable. Women flattered those better off and the almighty Occupation personnel, while merchants clung to them for business favors. Old values and concepts had crumbled in Japan, and there was yet to arise any new social or moral order.

> A pom-pom girl yawns
> O-shaped red
> Void within
> Darkness of soft flesh
>
> Her skin is grimy
> With scars on her knee
> She is tough
> Rejecting slander
>
> A pom-pom girl yawns
> Engulfing all
> In Japan there is no hole
> Deeper than that
>
> If it swallows clamor
> Of war criminals and liberalists
> There still will be room for them
> There still will be room for them[2]

Some intellectuals recalled with chagrin that less than a year before the Japanese had regarded Americans as devils or unforgivable enemies and, when they were defeated, they feared that Japanese women would be violated. Kaneko, too, had seen women terribly worried about their safety even in the countryside near Mount Fuji. He had heard that some women actually shaved their heads in an attempt to deter possible enemy advances. The majority of the Japanese, however, were simply relieved that the nightly air raids had come to an end,

and their main concern was how to stay alive. For many women, prostitution was the only means of survival, and for many
men a quick conversion of their political placards from
militarism to imported "democracy" was the sure way to make
a good living. Everyone was busy, and few lamented the
chameleon change of attitude of the Japanese.

For Kaneko it was a peculiar period of blankness. He was
supposed to feel emancipated from the devastating war and
from the stupidity of man, who carried it on. Yet, he could not
help feeling as if he were floating in the void created after the
object he had fought against was removed. The leftist writers,
some of whom greeted the end of the war in prison, were
quick in organizing themselves to publish their new journal,
The New Japanese Literature (Shin Nihon bungaku). The leftists took the Allied Occupation Forces as their emancipators.
They hailed them and, along with the liberals who timidly had
survived the war without being imprisoned, dreamed of a rosy
future for Japan to be built to their liking under the direction
of the Occupation authorities. For most, the Japanese leaders
of the past were categorically villains, and the Occupation
Forces were saviors. "Democracy" was the name of the game
for Communists and liberals alike. Kaneko thought that "one
hundred million Japanese" were again unanimously moving
in one direction. He did not quite understand.

In April 1946, Kaneko wrote an essay called "On the
Japanese" (*"Nihonjin ni tsuite"*) for the first number of the
Cosmos, the journal which Okamoto was instrumental in
launching:

> The war gave me the opportunity to reevaluate the Japanese, who,
> like a drifting cloud or flowing water, left no trace on either side of
> the mirror. I am learning a lesson.
> Now living with people who have no thoughts, who love to ap-
> preciate nature rather than to hate fellow men, and who float silently
> along in time, I feel both relieved and disappointed. If the Japanese
> had been like this before, perhaps I should not have toiled to write
> poems during the war. For, as soon as the war ended, they unanim-
> ously underwent such a transfiguration as to become Americans.[3]

The *Cosmos* was an appropriate medium in which to express Kaneko's sense of relief and disappointment with such
cynicism. One of the earliest to voice its own opinion in the

shambles of the world of letters, the *Cosmos* in its editorial statement outspokenly criticized the opportunists who went along with the military during the war and, when the war was over, began acting like messengers of world peace.[4] In this journal Okamoto wished to publish Kaneko's poems which he had read in draft at Kaneko's house near Mount Fuji before the end of the war. He hoped that Kaneko's "poems of resistance" would provide the journal a commanding position in postwar Japanese literature.

Despite the shortage of paper and printing facilities, various poetry journals were launched in succession, and they were read by the people, who had been starving for nonpropaganda literature. Both the publishers and the readers seemed satisfied with the freedom of the press which was enforced by the Occupation Forces. Besides the *Cosmos*, such journals as *Pure Poetry (Junsuishi)*, *Modern Poetry Forum (Kindai shien)*, *New Poetic School (Shinshi-ha)*, and *Utopia (Yūtopia)* were launched within one year after the end of the war. None of these journals, however, advocated a strong philosophy which would appeal to serious readers. *Pure Poetry*, for example, tried merely to reimport Paul Valéry. The reality of Japan was so harsh that the readers could not afford to indulge in a game of abstraction, and the journals had to cope with rapid inflation and financial problems rather than style and ideals. Nonetheless, the poetry journals of prewar days, the *Four Seasons* and the *Historical Course*, also resumed publication around the same time.

As these journals were published, celebrated prewar poets, such as Miyoshi and Nishiwaki also revived and published their major works. Takamura, who had written poems in praise of the emperor and in spiritual support of the war, wrote in 1947 *A Short History of the Ignorant Man (Angu shōden)*, which was an expression of the poet's regrets for his cooperation with the military. Conscientious Takamura retired to a hut in the mountains and lived like a hermit.

Kaneko returned to his Kichijōji house in July 1946. There was a curious void: a lack of the sense of belonging together, the kind of warmth that the family had enjoyed during the war in the cold village near Mount Fuji. Furthermore, Moncoco Cosmetics Company, which had long been the source of the family income, was quickly going out of business due to the unavailability of materials. Just at that time, an incident that Kaneko himself did not wish to write about apparently occurred. He met a young woman, Ōkōchi Reiko, with whom he lived for more than ten years.[5] It might be added that Michiyo suffered from a severe case of rheumatism and had become bedridden shortly before the incident.

Of the new poetry journals, Kaneko became affiliated with the one called the *Futurists of Japan* (*Nihon mirai-ha*), and contributed a few old poems to it in 1947 and 1948. He chose to do so, because the *Futurists of Japan* was created by a nonpartisan group of poets including those known as lyricists, Communists, and anarchists, and it looked agreeable to his taste. The journal proclaimed in its initial number that it would serve as "a common ground for all, based on love and sincerity," and published Dadaist Takahashi's works, too. This group's attitude was to grope and find some direction on a broad basis, encompassing many tendencies.

The public, now recovering from the initial shock of the country's defeat, wanted something substantial to satisfy their intellectual thirst. They wondered what had become of the elder writers they used to know and what postwar literature should be like. Their expectations were real and serious, and there emerged young writers who presented somber visions of life. Some of these young writers decided to join established poets' societies rather than to create their own, and gradually changed the character of the societies. *Pure Poetry*, for example, when joined by such poets as Tamura Ryūichi (1923-) and Ayukawa Nobuo (1920-), took on a new character as a sort of crusader of postwar poetry. Later, both Tamura and Ayukawa became the principal members of the Arechi group, which, with its journal the *Wasteland* (*Arechi*), was to exert a great influence in postwar Japanese poetry.

The young poets disagreed with the older poets primarily on one particular point: "What was the war for them?" For the young, the war was reality that had undeniably existed, bringing death to their contemporaries, and affected them profoundly: the very basis for what they were in the postwar period. The older poets' interpretation was that the war years were a "blank" in the history of Japanese poetry, a dormant period which good writers wished to erase memories of. For some, especially for those who studied European literature, the condition of Japan was comparable to the wasteland that was created in Europe after the First World War. They believed that poetry would rise from the ashes, the irredeemable sense of loss and despair, rather than from the remains of mere movements and thoughts of the prewar poets.

At that time, there was still another group of poets who were as critical of contemporary poetry as of wartime poetry. Giving itself an exotic name, the Matinée Poétique, this group claimed that the degeneration of Japanese poetry during the war was due mainly to the lack of definitive form. The Matinée Poétique saw the diversity in style and thought of contemporary poetry as being helplessly chaotic, and advocated the need for form and music in poetry. They rejected "eloquence" or wordiness in poetry and postulated that "a universal poetic form" must be sought in the tradition of lyrical poems in ancient Japan. The form they relied on, however, consisted of four stanzas of four, four, three, and three lines—a sonnet form. The Matinée Poétique's attempt at giving direction to postwar Japanese poetry failed, when both the older poet, Miyoshi, and the younger poet, Ayukawa, criticized the group's error in theory and its lack of understanding in poetry. Some members of the group switched to the novel and criticism.

The journal *Cosmos*, to which Kaneko occasionally contributed essays, ceased publication in October 1948. It had performed the role of a prosecutor of the war collaborators and, to a lesser degree, that of a mediator for the contemporary poets. For Kaneko it was not important to decide who really was responsible for the degeneration of poetry during the war. For him the argument as to whether there was a blank page in the history of modern Japanese poetry was of no significance. Young poets' recognition of a meaning in the wartime experience looked to him to be superficial. What did they produce out of the experience? Kaneko asked. It was indeed time for him to release his wartime works in book form, outside of the factional journals.

All the restrictions on publishing having been theoretically repealed, it appeared possible to publish books. However, many publishers were now profiting from the popularity of pornographic and nonsense literature, which filled the spiritual void of many people who had lost their direction.

Kaneko looked for a serious publisher willing to print his poems, but he found no one interested in all of the manuscripts he brought with him. Finally, in April 1948, Nihon Mirai Sha, the publisher of the *Futurists of Japan*, published a portion of the manuscripts. The book was *My Parachute (Rakkasan)*, which featured "My Parachute." Then, at very short intervals, other firms wanted to publish his wartime works. The Hokuto Shoin published *The Moth (Ga)* in September of the same year. In the following year Sōgensha in Ōsaka published *An Elegy for Women (Onna-tachi e no erejii)*, and Jūjiya published *The Song of the Devil's Son (Oni no ko no uta)*.

These books stood out in the contemporary world of poetry, not because of the antiwar sentiment in some poems or because of the works' apparent nonmodernistic style, but because of their straightforward descriptions of human conditions and unyielding probing into the nature of man, who created those conditions. Common to these books was a detached eye that observed all, and this eye belonged to the poet who was forever feeling lonesome—lonesome because he was alone and yet could not escape from being a part of everything.

Kaneko was not a lofty theoretician like Nishiwaki. Nor was he like the political poets who formed a clique and accused others of collaboration with the war or some such social evil. Kaneko's disappointment with man was at once mingled with his affection for man. His detachment was backed by his attachment. His spite was the other side of his love. He was both lonely and proud to be alone. And his language, different from current Japanese, which was being invaded by neologisms, was dignified by a touch of classicism. His lines and stanzas were so carefully constructed that, though seemingly unelaborate, they resonated to create a marvelous chain of imagery.

My Parachute includes a long poem called "The Song of Loneliness" ("*Sabishisa no uta*"), written toward the end of the war. It opens with:

> Where's it from—I mean, this loneliness?
> From her skin like evening glory?
> Complexion or retreating figure?
>
> Her threadlike heart?
> Or this scene
> Creating such a heart?

> The moonlight on a screen?
>
> Dead leaves on a mat?
>
> Loneliness,
> Creeping down the spine like moisture or mold,
> Rots the heart and oozes from our skin.
>
> Loneliness of bartered women,
> Or of orphans
> Raised in adversity.
>
> Or loneliness of those thinking it right
> To have form, but not a Self,
> Of claylike people.[6]

The woman introduced in the first stanza is not the love of the lonely man. She is a woman who was sold because of economic adversity or natural calamity, because of the traditional family system built on primogeniture, because of the conventions and old institutions, or because of her fate of being born female in Japan. She shone in the summer evening and wore her body and heart until they became like a thread. In the short successive stanzas, time passes from autumn, when the dim moonlight shines on a paper screen, to winter. Dead leaves crawl on straw mats in a drafty room. Loneliness oozes and spreads until it is equated with the desolate state of mind of those who have only "form, but not a Self." The poet is referring to the universal loneliness that permeates history. Like the master poets in ancient times, he treads in it.

> This loneliness might be smoke
> Of leaves burned in autumn,
> Water's quiet song,
> Season's steady change,
> Subtle movement of sprays,
> Shaking of rock, dying grass —
> All things that pass.
>
> Stepping in the reed thicket,
> No longer productive,
> Loneliness departs
> Toward clouds,
> At the chill of setting sun.

> Loneliness treads
> Looking for lodging
>
> Listening to the sound of the mountain,
> Through the night,
> I lie alone.
> In the empty *saké* bottle
> I hear the cry of a child I left at home.[7]

The second part of "The Song of Loneliness" opens with a reminder that the poet is a product of this loneliness. There is a fifty-year-old poet contemplating by the foggy shore of a lake. There is also a splendid summary of the history of Japan, which is viewed by the poet as passing from a misty mythological state to a cultured imperial state that maintained a harem. Except in a few scroll paintings by master artists, nowhere else can one find this precise history of Japan. In Japan, both courtiers and courtisans sang the song of loneliness.

> I was born in the fog
> Of this country's loneliness
>
> Fog hiding mountain and gorge,
> Thick vapor on the lake,
> Seals past and future;
> My half-century of life.
>
> My country:
> Loneliness alone fresh
> As fog rising endlessly.
>
> From loneliness
> We extract life's meaning
> And would write poetry.
>
> In loneliness
> We see palace flowers,
> Women wet with morning dew
> Picked at others' will,
> They bloom in shade.
>
> Their chapped lips and cheeks—
> I hear an unceasing prayer
> Resounding dark with their fate:
> A bunch of hair they left,
> And ropes that tied them down.

> They tuned loneliness
> And called it Yoshiwara Song.[8]

The Japanese were familiar with the sad tune of the song the
prostitutes in Yoshiwara sang at tedious hours. Kaneko knew it
too well, for he had sung it himself. It was the basic tune of
poetry in Japan, where he had lived. Kaneko's "The Song of
Loneliness" continues like the long lament of the Yoshiwara
prostitutes.

> Poverty after loneliness
> Paddy fields, peasant's misery
> Ignorance, resignation, and humility –
> From all these loneliness spreads.
>
> But, in the end, my loneliness
> Is that born here
> I grew and made friends in Japan,
> That I sit at a shabby table
> With soybean soup and rhubarb for breakfast
> And bamboo salad for dinner.
>
> That I, marching to my tomb,
> Transmit ancestral loneliness
> To my children, then lie dead.
>
> Knowing, after death
> Five, ten, a hundred
> Years from now
> Loneliness persists,
> Fog twenty times as thick
> Covering every corner of Japan,
> Rain then clearing.
>
> A sudden recollection of pain
> Of beautiful hills and rivers
> Entranced
> My heart is lost.[9]

The third part of "The Song of Loneliness" turns to the
Japanese of modern times, who drink coffee and smoke cigars.
It is not only in the traditional Japanese that Kaneko finds
loneliness. He discovers a root of loneliness in modern
Japanese, those who sit at an imported teak table with bread
and butter and talk of Western thought, those who are content

with having the unbroken line of Emperors. Kaneko mocks
that they still smell of the old Japanese-style toilet. "The
loneliness," the poet concludes, "finally caused the war." He
in fact witnessed many people "plucked like weeds," made to
leave mother and wife, "blinded by the Emperor's name," and
shipped out "like urchins." The fourth and last part of the
poem reads:

> Egoism; shallow affection.
> Women lined up for rations
> Patiently like beggars.
> I have never seen before
> Loneliness this deep, this intense,
> The end of a nation,
> In the sad complexion of the Japanese.
> But I care no more
> Such loneliness does not bother me.
>
> The loneliness of the lonely I,
> The true loneliness is no one beside me
> Resisting degeneration
> Willing to walk the other way
> To examine loneliness.
> Loneliness is that,
> And there is nothing beyond it.[10]

Does this loneliness match in depth that of the seventeenth-
century *haiku* master Basho, who wrote, "*Kono michi ya /
yukuhito nashi ni / aki no kure*" (On this road there is / No
one besides me; / Autumn ends)? There have been poets who
sang about their solitary positions in nature and recorded their
works in anthologies. There have also been poets who were
capable of equating their lonely hearts with the vastness of the
world, thereby creating a universal appeal in their poetry.
Kaneko's loneliness seems to lack such a sense of serenity,
satisfaction, or resignation. The loneliness of this poet has yet
to be fulfilled; it is a helpless, even desperate, loneliness derived from the horrible fact that there is no resonance of his
heartbeat outside of him. Still, Kaneko is euphemistic, so that
only careful readers notice that he has attached to this poem
Zarathustra's remark: "A state is called the coldest of all cold
monsters. Coldly lieth it also; and this lie creepeth from its
mouth: 'I, the state, am the people.'"

Kaneko did not believe in the fame that this and other collections of his poems brought to him. He was still "a seal who faces the other way" and wondered if this treatment was not the same in essence as that which the war supporters received during the war. What position, then, would the critics debating over wartime poetry give to him? No matter. Kaneko associated with many people, journals, and literary societies, but he never really became a member of any of them. Paradoxical as it may be, he was always outside of any literary movements. He had been apprehensive of men who, forming cliques without a Self, rushed fanatically to support some other's selfish choice and now were unanimously going for the "democracy" that was being implemented by the Occupation Forces. Kaneko was disappointed with people who lacked the Self. Often indignant with the evils brought about by such people, he saw the state of man to be tragic. He therefore entitled the collection of his postwar poems, to be published in 1952, *The Tragedy of Man (Ningen no higeki)*.

Kaneko's other collection during the years 1948 and 1949 also contained older works. *An Elegy for Women* of 1949 consisted, with a few exceptions, of the works written prior to the beginning of the Pacific War. Accordingly, the "women" whom Kaneko wrote about resembled those he met or saw in Southeast Asia: old women and shrewd young girls, both native and Japanese, who were traded as profitable commodities in Southeast Asia. In its subject matter and treatment, the works were comparable to "The Sharks" of 1937 and *The Journey through Malay and Dutch-India* of 1940 rather than to the other books published together in the postwar period. The surface scenes of the prostitutes, "slave" traders, ports, and palm trees were not unrelated to the poet's critical attitude toward colonialism and the social system which caused the misery of the women. There was a sorrowful, sympathetic eye of the observer. It must not be missed, however, that there was also, as in "The Sharks" and *The Journey through Malay and Dutch-India*, the poet's soul wandering from port to port, from loneliness to loneliness, from woman to woman. The poet called these poems "elegies," not "songs." The Japanese journalist who sarcastically reported that Kaneko played the drums in an Indian port city could have been right. Perhaps Kaneko played the drums in tune with his elegy to pacify his

wandering soul. Read, for example, the following excerpt from
"Palm Trees Growing in Water" (*"Nippa yashi no uta"*),
which is only deceptively simple:

Upright
Palm trees
Wanderer's companions
With long lashes
Wet with tears

My oar
Combing palms
Along the canoe
A snake swims

Up the Bandjarmasin
Down to Batu Pahat
Palms on the bank

My thoughts
On flowing water
Eternal friends

Faint light from civilization
Shines on a drifter from civilization
Of planters
Of spices and rubber

"It is best
Not to return"
Maxim of wandering

Palm trees
Sweeter than lovers
Or women
Who smoke in bed

Palm trees
In tired dispositions
Actually healthy, realistic
And smart
With no sign of corruption
Awefully pure
Showing off clean napes[11]

The Moth of 1948 and *The Song of the Devil's Son* of 1949,
both written during the Pacific War, did include the kind of
works which some critics labeled "poems of resistance." Here
is an excerpt from the one called "Night" ("*Yoru*"), selected
from *The Moth*.

> Alas, the ambitions
> Of the nineteenth century
> Pulled man out of the dark
> Like shelling oysters.
>
> The twentieth century
> Is pitiably naked.
> No thought, nor promise
> Keeps man warm.
>
> Dragged around
> Without a direction,
> We aren't allowed
> Even to ask why.
>
> We hear instead
> Pisa fell and Vienna burnt
> Day and night.
>
> Over the pine grove
> We see a flock of Boeings
> Going to destroy Tokyo.
>
> Tonight, however,
> No bombing.
> Dead tired silence.
> The pine grove looking ominous.
>
> The crescent moon.
> Darkness melts
> The aura—a sleepy eye.[12]

Kaneko, weary of nightly air raids, sustains the war, the darkness of the century, the tragedy of man. What there is is not
resignation, but anger. *The Moth* contains more works which
are more obviously "antiwar." The poet angrily shouts, "Burn
draft records / So no one can tell that I have a son," in "Mount
Fuji" ("*Fuji*"), and "War, don't you ever / Break this perfect

ring, the crystal of three of us," in "Three Points" ("*Santen*").
However, neither the world of *The Moth* nor that of *The Song
of the Devil's Son* is really far from *My Parachute*, which featured "The Song of Loneliness." What might look to some to
be "antiwar" and "camouflage to conceal his opposition" is
the technique necessary to enable him to reach beneath the
surface of reality during the war. For Kaneko, war, of all
human phenomena, is the utmost manifestation of stupidity,
weakness, and loneliness. Alone in dark times, Kaneko sang
about it.

"The Moth," in *The Moth*, which is as long and as grand in
scale as the earlier work, "The Sharks," offers the dark world
of the moon and cold night rather than the glaring sun and the
tropical sea. Here, the poet moves into the shady side of humanity, such as fatigue, sufferings, and disappointment.

Moth,
Why so? Already tired at birth,
Tentacles on head, powder on body, time's weight on shoulders,
You perch, puffing, trembling wings.

Dreams are broken, fingers clinging: the end of coquetry.
    Deceived by the far-off grandeur – yesterday's sunset.
    Momentary is the pleasure of the lured. Moth.
Where can you go?

A dark span of bushes and trees; the trapped cling to each other.
Permeating sense of doom. A moonless night.[13]

Like a meandering moth, the poet drifts through the silent
woods, "a thicket of grasses," in his lonesome attempt at finding beauty and, possibly, unfolding the layers of its secret. He
observes a moth sliding in the mirrorlike darkness. The dim
moonlight shines on its wings. Is the moth beauty? Or is it
death?

Powder on the mirror;
Dust from the moth. It is death:
Soft eternal body transparent like wax.[14]

The poet inadvertently stumbles on the moth's body, which is
still soft. What is beyond the body? Can he find beauty there
and overcome his loneliness? In the poem it is as if an old

flickering film continues its projection. He floats in thin air, where he resembles the moth, and the pine grove below looks like a hollow.

You, whom I have awaited, where are you?
    Spirited away or melted in the moon?
I cannot find you, but I know
    You are shining in an unexpected place
Like a jewel in the river's bottom.

You have taught me a passageway to heaven.
    The loneliness of love.[15]

Each of the eight parts of "The Moth" is considered to show the moth in a different posture in a different background at a different time. The true form of the moth cannot be easily identified, and the poet continues to search. After a long journey, he is lost and suddenly he wonders if he can return. He has indeed come a long way.

Flickering scenes, take me back, won't you?
To Florida, islands in the tropics, where there is no war.

In my binoculars I see only the Arctic, uninhabited, sleeting;
The sad, retreating figure of Chaplin fidgeting with a cane on the
    enormous whale, endlessly drifting.[16]

The image lingers and time fuses: the past seems to be in the present. "The Moth" is shadowy, slow-moving, and mysterious. Yet, Kaneko uses unusually difficult vocabulary that defies translation into other languages, as if to reminisce about the glistening palace of aesthetics in *A May Beetle*. This contrast of the subtle content to the hard shell amplifies the vastness and complexity of the world in which beauty and the war, and the poet and the moth, must coexist.

The moth knows it is watched, crawls shyly . . .
    without a faint noise. Only the feel.

Approaching like a wick burning out, flapping its wings like the last
    flame,
The moth falls in man's void and stays there in repose.
The moth is not a number. It is.a negative.

Its beauty—a sensation of depravity, not the casting of the worm.
The lonesome feast of life, violated, hurt, abandoned and stamped
  upon.[17]

Kaneko's imagery is manifold. He writes toward the end of the
poem, "The moth. It is a woman. / Wings broken due to noc-
turnal lewdness." The amorphous world of *The Moth* man-
ifests the darkness of the times and the loneliness of the poet
who lived in it.

  The Song of the Devil's Son of 1949 also contains some
"poems of resistance," but the book is clearly of a different
intent. In one of the poems, entitled "The Birth of the Devil's
Son" ("*Oni no ko no tanjō*"), Kaneko writes about "the devil."

The devil was born.
Hear the first cry? Such a dissatisfied tone,
To nourish the horrible teaching it suckled
At its mother's shriveled breasts.
The child with horns and a tail
Slept like a drunkard.

The devil came. Neighbors gathered
In front of the barn
Scorning, cursing, pointing fingers at him.

This scene is distorted, stained and smeared with the hackneyed
  thought.
Horseflies swarm heaven.
Seasons suffocate, the earth is damp,
The sun eclipses, ash falls on tin roof.
Everywhere poverty strikes
Only the mute, the deaf, the yellow and the paralytic.[18]

A subsequent poem, "The Wandering of the Devil's Son"
("*Oni no ko hōrō*"), has the caption, "Fifty years after the devil's son hatched," and it explains de facto that the devil is a
wandering poet. Yet, the poem ends with the vexing line,
"The devil's son is not me, but you!"

  One critic defined the devil's son as "something unclear,
which might be termed a malformed child born out of
Kaneko's fantasy."[19] Another disputed this and redefined the
devil's son as "Christ himself."[20] Trying to define Kaneko's
devil is as useless as quarreling over the frequency of mention

of a particular girl's name in *An Elegy for Women*. The shark shows many different faces, and so does the moth. In *The Song of the Devil's Son* the devil appears in the poet's nostril, in Japanese folk tales, in the ghosts of the war dead, in the people who mourn death, and in the underworld into which the poet wanders. This devil, like a ghost, has the ability to transfigure itself so it assumes various personages before the reader.

At that time, Japan was disturbed by a series of mysterious accidents, which cast a dark shadow over the minds of the people who were trying to reconstruct the country. The accidents, all occurring in 1949, involved the National Railway, where, whether relevant to the accidents or not, labor unions were very strong and strikes were frequent. Once a train was derailed. Another time, a high-ranking National Railway Corporation director was found dead on a track. There was also a rear-end collision, killing many passengers. In all these cases, causes were not found and they became political issues, resulting in legislative investigations. In some sectors of the country, there were rumors connecting the accidents and deaths to the intelligence activities of the Occupation Forces, which disliked the sizable advances of the Japanese Communist party at a national parliamentary election earlier that year. The leftists, whose sabotage and strikes had been smashed, were now saying that the Occupation Forces were not emancipators, but "American devils" of the wartime. In the ideological confusion, they saw the successful experiment of the atom bomb in the Soviet Union and the triumphant Communist revolution in China, both in the latter half of 1949.

In December 1949 the *Cosmos* resumed publication, immediately attacking, as before, "the poverty of poetic spirit which depended only on poets' experience, emotion, and political ideology, instead of filtering them."[21] According to the *Cosmos*, contemporary Japanese poetry was no different from wartime poems in that "the forbearance, joy, sorrow, hope and determination" of the poets were regimented exactly as in the war. To this journal, too, Kaneko contributed a few miscellaneous essays entitled "Cosmos Miscellany" ("*Kosumosu zakki*"). These nonpolitical essays were on the poets of the past and on his old friends.

Kaneko's involvement with Ōkōchi Reiko was presumably continuing, while Michiyo continued to be bedridden because of the rheumatism that affected her entire body. One bright event was Ken's graduation from the Literature Department of Waseda University in 1950. Kaneko's old friend Hatanaka of the Chūō Kōron Publishing Company later revealed that Kaneko accompanied Ken to see him and asked him to find a job for Ken in the publishing business.[22] Kaneko was pleased by the fact that Ken did not choose to be a poet; he disliked the idea that Ken, like himself, might suffer from poverty.[23] But Hatanaka advised Ken against entering business and persuaded him to further his study of French at a graduate school. The time was before the Korean War, when jobs were still scarce and wages were low in Japan. Kaneko, who by nature disliked the academic, neither agreed nor disagreed with Hatanaka. He listened to him in silence.

Before Kaneko published his "first" collection of postwar poems, *The Tragedy of Man*, his reputation had been established as "poet of resistance." Some critics compared Kaneko to such French poets as Louis Aragon and Paul Eluard, who engaged in the resistance movement against the Nazis during the Second World War. They also pointed out that Kaneko's work would nicely fill the gap between the socialist poems of the prewar days and the Communists', farmers', and factory workers' poems in postwar Japan, completing the line of historical development of modern Japanese poetry. Kaneko was indifferent to such a niche for himself in the arrangement of other poets. Nor was he much concerned with the current activities of new groups of writers. It was the time when well-known leftist novelists like Abe Kōbō (1924-), Shiina Rinzō (1911-), and Noma Hiroshi (1915-) joined the leading poetry journal, *Archipelago* (*Rettō*), and greatly expanded the leftist literature in Japan.

Kaneko published three books of translated French poetry during 1951 and 1952. One of the books was Louis Aragon's, and the others were of the poets whom he envied or admired: Rimbaud and Baudelaire. While he wished to be like Rimbaud, who quit poetry at twenty and concentrated the rest of his brief life on making money, Kaneko was apparently preoccupied with Baudelaire's favorite themes, such as "journey," "prostitution," "decomposition," and "ghosts."

The Tragedy of Man of 1952, a long poem consisting of ten parts, opens with a section on the theme of "journey," sings about postwar prostitutes in "The Song of a Pom-pom Girl," quoted earlier, and continues on to depict the decomposed body of a ninth-century Japanese poetess. In its preface, however, Kaneko specifies that *The Tragedy of Man* is an "autobiography" of the poet which overlaps the tragic history of man. Kaneko sees man as a "ghost," which, like the devil and his son in *The Song of the Devil's Son*, takes on many different forms. For example:

> The ghost waited
> While I wrote. Patiently
> Behind me he was
> Reading my writing!
>
> The ghost. Cotton dust.
> Fallen hair. Whatever,
> Like a stain on a curtain
> It is an indefinable something.[24]

This ghost resembles that of *Les Fleurs du Mal*. If you want to unmask him, the poet advises the reader, you must follow him, "journeying on a sandy beach, in winter, stepping on dry shells." In this book, Kaneko pursues him into "a dark pavillion like a warehouse" and studies him to unfold the true nature of man.

The fifty-seven-year-old poet claims that he is awakened in the ruins of Tokyo, convinced that all values in life are relative and only death is absolute. Death is, the poet asserts, at least sincere and respectable: it is in fact man's only worthy achievement. In Kaneko's conception, therefore, there is a realm between the relative and the absolute, where the living-dead who are indistinguishable either from the living or from the dead reside. Those who are in between are Kaneko's devils, ghosts—the people who, lacking the Self, constitute "the state . . . the coldest of all cold monsters." The poet despises them. Sometimes, he fears them. He tries to ignore them. Too often, however, he must beg them for mercy, because there are places in this world of man where it is difficult to pass without their help. And that is man's tragedy.

> There are barriers hard to pass
> Unless we beg the ghosts

> To please carry our cases. As we are
> We are helpless as curs.
>
> What we think of as being lonely
> Is being alone with the ghosts.
> Our ignorance: existence is a useless check
> That we received from the ghosts.[25]

From the ancient period of rulers and heroes to the modern times of the masses, man's history had been written by "the ghosts," so that, Kaneko believed, no value was absolute. In the world of politics and poetics alike, there were the same kind of Self-less people acting as leaders. Some rightists before the war were active on the left in the postwar period and were afraid of "the red purge" by the Occupation Authorities. The others behaved as if they had been liberal throughout. The Occupation Forces that had once banned censorship were now examining every Japanese publication. *Kinkakuji*, the temple of golden pavillion in Kyoto which had been regarded as a symbol of eternity, burned to the ground, and soon the Supreme Commander of the Allied Occupation Forces, General Douglas MacArthur, was dismissed. Japan, which had proclaimed a complete disarmament under the new Constitution, now had a small army and her industry began producing arms again. The ghosts drove man, who accepted their bidding as his fate. Driven by the ghosts, the poet, too, had aged. Before he knew it, about fifty years had passed. Kaneko's figure was suddenly old.

> With the loafers in this world
> Doing little for fifty years
> Drop by drop I fell
> From a chipped bowl
>
> To obtain peace of mind
> I tried to grasp death
> I still don't get it
> Death annoys me all the same
>
> Watching myself wither
> I grow doubly tired
> For us lucky or unlucky
> Death awaits anyway

> To a cold-sensitive body
> Clinging till the end
> Is a pair of testicles
> Like an eighty-year-old's[26]

Part Three of *The Tragedy of Man*, which includes the above, is subtitled "About Death" ("*Shi ni tsuite*"). It is not that the poet has not accepted death and is afraid of it. He is keenly aware that he has lived more than fifty years and still expects, with a certain apprehension, that his life must undergo many more changes.

The same part of the book contains the poet's memory of a picture scroll depicting the life of Ono no Komachi, the legendary poetess of the ninth century, which he had seen in Sōtarō's art collection. Entitled *The Komachi Transfiguration* (*Komachi hensō no zu*), the scroll illustrated different stages of beautiful Komachi's life: the aged poetess being lonesome, forgotten, fallen by the roadside, eaten by maggots, picked by birds, pierced by pampas grass, and scattered by the wind. The scroll was a manifestation of the Buddhist belief in the transfiguration of all things, from birth, through death, to nothingness—all things will pass, turn to matter, and then be reborn. In Kaneko's mind the grotesque pictures overlapped the fantasy worlds of Baudelaire and of Bosch. Komachi's beauty turned to nothingness, but her poems remain. Baudelaire was under the gravestone in Montparnasse, where he had visited, but his poetry had haunted him and will continue to do so. What, then, is death? Is it merely an unlucky lottery number for the one who bought it? Is it a permanent bankruptcy for the dead and a complete purge for those surrounding the dead? What will happen to his art after his death? Kaneko ponders:

> A sage emperor in ancient times
> Set fire to every book
> Words surviving for a thousand years
> Are like phantoms indeed
>
> Only momentarily can we
> Recall the fragrance and warmth
> Of a beautiful dress cast off
> By a woman who no longer exists

After friends and lovers die
And I too vanish
If only my heart—my book—remains
How grotesque it will be

Sordid temptation
Of wishing to preserve
Fame and books
No other cruelty exists[27]

It was a fallacy for Kaneko to argue about how the recent history of Japanese poetry should be written. He had seen many incidents where values and concepts were changed by the "ghosts." It is a cruel act, Kaneko declares, to let the poet's books be subjected to the judgment of the chameleonlike people after his death.

Parts Five, Six, and Seven of *The Tragedy of Man* turn to postwar Japan, where the work's greatest concern lies. Kaneko adds a caption to Part Five, which reads, "The day when the world is finally freed from man and his prejudice—the Christians call it Judgment Day," and Kaneko is of course no Christian. His analogy here is bitterly sharp. He depicts American jeeps running around, raising dust, and "phalli," some with anchor-pattern tattoos, sticking out of the ruins. The jeep was an amazing machine for the Japanese whose main means of transportation at the time was the freight train. The "phalli" is a metaphor for tall, Popeye-like GIs who stalked about Japanese cities. Next to the jeeps and "phalli" are "pom-pom girls" and mulatto babies. The poem also depicts a cave in the ruins, no doubt an old bomb shelter, where the poet meets a mad woman who shows him her "past"—a sewing box, a mirror, and a musical instrument—all evidences of her noble upbringing, neatly stored. In the next part of the poem, this woman is a "pom-pom" who claims that she is a descendant of an emperor and that her father was a director of a large bank. When yesterday's enemy is today's ruler, women who were chaste before the war stand on the street corners, and militarists easily become pacifists. Even the emperor and the Supreme Commander of the Allied Powers lose their power, and the respectable poet Takamura is condemned, whereas Miyazawa Kenji (1896-1933) is uncovered from obscurity and made a very famous poet. After all, what is permanent? Is there such a thing as an eternal art in this world? Whatever the answers may be, man must live, and that is the tragedy of man.

The setting shifts from Tokyo to the sea, and Kaneko opens Part Eight with a poem called "Christ Roaming the Bottom of the Sea" (*"Kaitei o samayou Kirisuto"*), which begins with:

> Christ?
> You don't know it?
> He's merely a deformed fetus.[28]

And Kaneko asks, "For how many centuries has man carried that naked man on the cross?" Today Christ is still sought after: cameras are directed at him and shutters are clicked. He is interviewed: "Why are you naked in this cold weather?" Christ answers, "I'm suffering for man." Then, the poet cuts in to refute: "I'll tell you why. It's because you cannot think of any means to hide your lie." Christ blushes and in extreme embarrassment murmurs, "I have just come out of the sea. How do you know me so well?" To Kaneko, Christ is no different from Vasco da Gama, Singapore's Mayor Clifford, or, for that matter, any soldier who came to Japan as conquerer. Or, is he the poet still roaming the sea like a ghostlike jellyfish, as in "The Song of a Jellyfish" (*"Kurage no uta"*)?

The Song of a Jellyfish

> Tossed and thrown
> Pushed aside
> I finally became
> Transparent like this.
>
> It has not been an easy life, you know.
>
> Can you see from there?
> In my stomach
> An old toothbrush
> And yellow liquid.
>
> How could my heart
> Have stood this, you ask?
> My heart with my guts
> Left me for the waves.
>
> What is this, then?
> Me. Jelly.

Emptiness tossed up
And thrown back again.

Once folded
Then blooming
Like a purple flower,
Lighting myself at night.

No, what is being tossed about
Is only my heart that has lost my body.
A thin wrapper
Covering my heart.

No, not even that.
It's only a shadow
Of my agony, tired
Of having been tossed about for so long.[29]

The Tragedy of Man was awarded the Yomiuri Literary Prize in 1953. In the same year, Kaneko began to work again for a cosmetics company which was managed by the same people who had run Moncoco. Ken, now in graduate school, was hoping to go to France to advance his study. Kaneko needed money to support his family, Ōkochi, and himself. He saw many younger poets were now obtaining fancy jobs, such as teaching and editing, and producing poems on the side, while leading a comfortable life. Men who lived for poetry, people who enjoyed poetry in poverty, poets who lived poetry were disappearing in Japan.

The economy of the country was benefiting from the Korean War, for which Japan served as a supply depot for the U.N. Military. The terrible shortage of materials, which had forced Moncoco and numerous other companies to go out of business, was being eased. Inflation seemed to be advancing at a slower rate than before, and labor disputes and strikes were fewer. The public quickly forgot that Hara Tamiki (1905-1951), the novelist who survived the atomic bomb attack in Hiroshima, had killed himself in fear of another atomic bombing at the outbreak of the Korean War.

By that time, Kaneko's writings had irritated the critics of the left. His position as neither Communist nor anarchist invited jealousy and criticism. The members of the New Japan

Literary Society, which published the journal the *New Japanese Literature* under the guidance of the Japanese Communist party, had had high hopes of having Kaneko on their side. They found Kaneko's wartime poems not in disagreement with their political beliefs: in fact, they found them perfectly fitted to their purpose. The truth was that they had noticed through the debate on wartime Japanese poetry that their literary output during the war was as "blank" as that of the old liberal writers whom they attacked, and they needed their own "poems of resistance" as a proof of their continued fight against fascism. Even the hard-core members of the society, such as Nakano and Tsuboi, did not have quality "resistance" works to show to the world. In 1949, therefore, the society compiled an anthology of poems by Nakano, Oguma Hideo (1901-1940), and Kaneko in their attempt at filling their "blank" in the history of leftist literature in Japan. Clearly, however, Kaneko was too much a nonpartisan vagabond to be ranked in the hierarchy of the left.

In 1951, Tsuboi Shigeji (1898-   ), a foremost anarchist-turned-Marxist, criticized Kaneko, arguing that Kaneko's postwar works were several grades lower in quality than "The Sharks," while praising "The Sharks." The members of the Japanese Communist party, severely reprimanded by the Cominform in 1950, were confused. In the January 1955 issue of *Modern Poetry* (*Gendaishi*), Okamoto published an open letter to Kaneko, in which he attacked Kaneko in the same vein as those of the New Japan Literary Society. He denounced Kaneko's postwar poems, saying that they merely narrated, in Kaneko's own talkative way, his "view of life or some such insignificant whim."[30]

Later, when Okamoto published his book of poetry, Kaneko wrote a review, in which he touched on Okamoto's open letter:

I appreciated your criticism. But, Okamoto, did you not overestimate me? Your displeasure seemed to me derived from it. Actually, I am an unorganized, lazy man, so that I don't care much about anything, unless, of course, it is about something very unjust. The responsibility and reputation that the world has given me don't suit me at all. I am willing to take off my label of poet and give it to anyone who wants it. If I can find some other job, that is.[31]

Kaneko was approaching the age of sixty. He recalled that Yokomitsu was only fifty when he died; that his old friend Fukushi and his longtime supporter Satō Kōroku had both died. Momota died, too. Tanizaki was active, but Kaneko had lost contact with him. He noticed that various local magazines were being launched and new, energetic writers were advancing on to more prestigious, established journals. The new writers would not believe him, Kaneko thought, if he told them that he was as youthful as they at heart.

Kaneko asked the old poet Kawaji, whom he had asked nearly forty years before to help publish his first collection of poems, *The House of Earthen Walls*, to write a postscript for a new collection of poems. The collection, entitled *Inhumanity* (*Hijō*), was published in 1955, with Kawaji's essay. Kawaji wrote:

> You [Kaneko] are extraordinarily sensitive and yet vigorous. You are even talkative, though not overly. Sentimentalism has no place in you. You reject abstraction and point to the heart of the matter. You write to subdue your anger, saying that you take up your pen only when you are angry. It is wondrous that poetry is a pacifier for you.
>
> We modern men are not content. If we are to live sincerely, we must confront hypocrisy, falsehood and vanity. You disclose these vices in your poems. Some might think that you are unrestrained, but what you show to us is nothing other than today's chaotic reality. You probe into matter and convert filth and blood into poetry. You are a remarkable man. . . . In *Hijō* you showed us the man who calmly lives in this world of pain, while despising and sharply attacking it. This is a great achievement. *Hijō*, which is uniquely yours, represents the breadth and depth of modern Japanese poetry.[32]

The title of the book, "Hijō," commonly means "unemotional" and, by extension, conveys the meaning "callous," "heartless," and even "cruel." What Kaneko meant by this, however, was rather "non-emotional," signifying the state of mind that transcended the ordinary emotions, such as love and hate. He was referring to the mind of an accomplished poet who, after having experienced joy, sorrow, and all, attained a true undertanding of life, as in the following poem.

IDEA

Living is constant restraint
Bearing the tensions – I know,

But the world is so incredibly askew I can hardly stand.
In the slime of moss and fish, I am like a beginning skater;
Slipping and clinging,

Irritated. I exhaust my life's energy to carry a cup of coffee,
Without spilling it, to such a remote table.

And hecklers shout, some near my ear,
"No one will be there even if you make it,"
Striking me with the idea that my efforts will be in vain.[33]

If this poem does not show "the breadth and depth of modern Japanese poetry," as Kawaji remarked, it does show the height that Kaneko attained. Each of the three stanzas is grammatically incomplete, intensifying the sense of the instability of the world and precariousness of the poet's position in the world, and modifies the following stanza until the tension mounts to a release in the final line. The skewed world does not pardon the tired, old poet, who is about to finish carrying a cup of coffee across the world without spilling it. Kaneko is saying that his life is like a clumsy waiter's: after all his trouble, he is laughed at. There is cynicism. There is even humor: the poet, perhaps wearing a frock coat like Chaplin's, is jeered at by the audience. Kaneko entitles this work "IDEA," using English in capital letters. Whose IDEA is this? A kind of Divine Providence, the poem "IDEA" is the essence of *hijō*, or inhumanity.

This idea that the poet's work is ultimately unrewarding except for himself is also expressed in the following poem, "Petal" (*"Hanabira"*).

Petal

Like a juggler, I balanced beams of trust
    On a crafty heart—air vibrations.

Life's pit: the audience deemed me
    A success.

Until today, eating free meals,
    Making my heart throb,

Even wounding myself, a dagger in my sleeve,
    I kept it with me—my petal

I tore and crumpled it to wipe my nose, chewed and spat,
  And though horrible, stuffed it in a pipe to breathe its smoke.[34]

The restaurant waiter in the previous poem is a circus man in
this poem. It has been a precarious life, the poet says, trying
not to fail in his act as a juggler. Often wounding himself with
a dagger, however, he has managed to keep a flower. The petal
is of course poetry, which he smokes in order to perpetuate it.
Kaneko is like the Zen monk who epitomized all the teachings
in one question: "A dragon ate the universe. Where are the
mountains and rivers?"

In most branches of Japanese art, the state of complete
maturity is termed "kareta," which means "weathered,"
"withered," or "dry." This is the state which an artist, compared to a tree in nature, could reach only after passing
through the periods of growth, from buds to blooming flowers,
from fruit-bearing to dry branches against the clear wintry sky.
Only then is the tree free from nature's threat, putting all
memories of love and hate into its dendro-chronology. In Zen
Buddhism, this state is enlightenment, the highest level of
understanding man can reach. The poems in Inhumanity are
"weathered," indicating Kaneko's accomplished artistry. Here
is another:

AMITIÉ

Rarely do I look back; the Past
Is a vast expanse and at its end is you, my friend.
It was there in the mist where I met one like you.

The direction of the past, faded, like the color of a wilted rose,
Opens like an abandoned field by the sea.

Ah, how happy I'd be if I could just watch the scenery.
—Time, why are you in such a hurry?—
We'll be going anyway;

I'll put my hand on your shoulder,
In an unfinished form called Fate. Lingering in my mind
Is a dark sea bottom with a casket lid: the plain covered
by a flurry of butterflies.[35]

   Kaneko lived twenty more prolific years after the completion of *Inhumanity*. His final two decades, however, seemed
somewhat relaxed when compared with the intensity of his
first sixty years leading up to *Inhumanity*. Perhaps only after
he reached the state of *hijō*, transcending love and hate, could
he start writing his autobiographies, serving as "critic" of
poems contributed to magazines, attending round-table discussions, talking about eroticism, women, and his experience
with women, and acquiring his name in the mass media as
"*Ero jiisan*," or the erotic old man.

> Fifty some years
> Passed by me
> A vast stretch
> To the far-off reeds
>
> Seems boundless indeed
> But right there
> Things happened
> Certain events
>
> Resembling water
> Washed by time
> Undercurrent
> That trips
>
> Love and hate
> As they tangle
> Now rising then falling
> I had no time to enjoy
>
> Do not be surprised
> Women
> Except for your sweetness
> All have been petty
>
> Empty like wind
> Blowing through the reeds
> From leaves
> To leaves
>
> A slender woman
> Like a stalk

In a glass
Reaches out smiling

Not to touch me
Without looking back
Women went by
They all were flowers

Water
Carried them
Destination
Unknown

Lightness
Of my shell
Remained
After fifty years

Clarity
Ask my heart
Floating down the river
If any revolting spirit is left[36]

Entitled "The Reeds" ("*Ashi*"), this poem presents a vast horizontal picture of a river where reeds are growing. There is a boat, flowing as water flows, with the poet in it. Toward the end of the expanse is a hazy area where water and sky are one. The poet can hardly believe that in this soft milky scenery, in his past, some fifty years of time have elapsed. The fact is, Kaneko knows, that some things did happen in the space between the water and the sky. There were wars and revolution. There were always women. From the small boat, however, everything looks vague and insubstantial. Was not everything like the mirage that disappears with the wind? Perhaps, except for the sweetness of the women. All those women who had been kind to him were flowers. But where are they now? They too have been carried far by the river. The poet realizes how free he is, how light his heart is, and how lonely he still is.

It is possible to compare these poems to the *renga*, or linked-verse of medieval Japan. The stanzas are uniform and short, and they appear to lack significance individually. But they are linked by means of association and progression, and they form a flow of emotions or a set of pictures. Like good *renga*, they could be appreciated in parts as well as in their entirety. The following is a poem which Kaneko called "Inhumanity" *("Hijō)* in his book *Inhumanity*.

Inhumanity

The scenery, having emerged softly from darkness,
Is unconscious like a dreaming child in a vignette.

The mist rises, scattering. Clumps of reeds,
Swaying in the morning air, drift down the river.

How sternly the day begins among the sleepy faces!
But youth is severe. Touching the heart,

He hurts others, himself blood-stained like the reeds.
Even more miserable than I, the remains of youth.

My patched heart is an overripe fruit,
Picked by birds, ready to fall.

I must die, it seems, to vacate my shaky chair, my old crutches
On the muddy bank, Japan is so crowded.

But death is as difficult as life.
Clouding the rouge-dyed water.

I have worked reluctantly. For food, first,
Then I poked aimlessly around a sunken ship,

As if in search of a drowned man. I also chased
The water birds flying behind the withered reeds.

In today's world of spite,
When adultery is committed to forgive, killing to assert

Those lovers and dreamers of life seem immature
Like children unable to give up a favorite toy.

The reeds grow densely, now terrified, noisy,
Now still, stupified, encircling us completely.

Making ripples in our homeland, devastated Japan
Like a salamander on the marsh bottom,

Every spring, precisely, the reeds sprouted green buds.
Ah, the prosperous allow no space

Among the dead leaves, broken stalks and deserted mats.
Which burden is heavier, our misfortune of the '40s

Or the youth of the '50s? Whichever, the world is
Filled with the clamor of Yanks and uncivilized men

The world's new enterprisers, pouring cement down our backs,
Between our individualities, make us realize that we are surrounded

By a stone wall, that we are useless if not consumed by the bunch.
Paving "death" over the clumps of reeds, pale, irritated faces,

Over those trying to escape fate, those discontented,
They pervade, enormous INHUMANITY.

Thus night spreads, from where I stand;
Man's darkness begins. And the reeds burn,

Scattering the sparks on the limbs of the fleeing
Whose hair is already afire. Burning,

Yes, the reeds are searching. As far as the fire illuminates,
Through the veins of the layered leaves,

They try to ascertain something remote,
Too far to gain, that never changes:

The moment of blank before the appearance of a god
Totally different from the old gods, the soul's void

So clearly illumined by lightning in the dark.
And burning trucks at the edge of a glistening pavement.

The reeds all around this
Are immersed in the dark sky.
The stars are especially
Bright tonight.

A gentle breeze passes
Over the reeds;
The stars twinkle
In the distance.

A shooting star—
Is a burning match
An outcast tossed
Into the dark night.[37]

CHAPTER 5

Appraisal: 1957-1975

K ANEKO had started the installations of "Autobiography" ("*Jiden*") for the poetry magazine *Eureka* (*Yuriika*) in December 1956. After its completion, he republished it as a book under a new title, *The Poet* (*Shijin*), in 1957. He had previously demonstrated his ability in prose through prose poems, various essays, and *The Journey through Malay and Dutch-India*. In a more refined and dignified style, *The Poet* narrated the author's life, which could not possibly be repeated because of the singularity of his love for poetry and life. While the work was generally factual, it abounded with poetic assertions of his Self.

For this book, Kaneko wrote a postscript, which contained the following:

> The word "*shijin*" [poet] has come to mean a man who is looking up at the sky gaping like a fool, after his purity has been corrupted and his sensitivity destroyed. The poet from now on should not be like him. This poet learned this through sixty years of toil, and now I am making a fresh start.[1]

Kaneko concluded this postscript with a sarcastic note, saying that the Japanese script for "poetry," composed of two radicals meaning "words" and "temple" respectively, smelled to him of incense in a religious sanctuary. The essence of poetry, he mused, might be something strange, not worthy to be man's life work. He went on to write that he did not enter into a religious field because he was not conceited enough to preach, and he was not presumptuous enough to work in a political or educational field. Of the other fields, he noted that business was cheating and science awesome. Kaneko was conversely saying that he could not have been anything but a poet and he would continue to be so. In other words, *The Poet* was Kaneko's renewed pronouncement of his intention to pursue his poetry.

On the other hand, Kaneko believed that one long cycle had come to an end as he looked back over his sixty years of life in his autobiography; that *Inhumanity* of 1955 had been a landmark in his life. He somberly entitled the last chapter of this autobiography "Making a Fresh Start" ("*Futatabi furidashi kara shuppatsu*"). *The Poet* was also the beginning of his task of summing up the past. In fact, he was to publish many other autobiographical works from this time on.

Poets' autobiographies were rare in Japan. Especially unique was the kind written by a poet who had roamed Southeast Asia and Europe and who had been consistent with his belief for the three troubled periods of prewar, wartime, and postwar. Some poets were conscious of their shifts in ideological stance so that, out of their sense of shame, they avoided writing about themselves. As Kaneko's autobiography progressed, even those who had not known him paid attention to him. Those who had liked his poems increased their understanding of and respect for them. Some expressed their amazement at the discovery that such a man as Kaneko existed in the same generation to which Hagiwara, Takamura, Nishiwaki, Miyoshi, and others belonged. Most admired the simple, beautiful, penetrating style of *The Poet*.

Subsequently, serious studies of Kaneko appeared at an increased rate. Until that time, Kaneko had been treated mostly in parts of books, along with other poets, or in connection with individual poems like "The Sharks." In 1957 the journal *Eureka* devoted one issue to the study of Kaneko and publishers' and editors' requests for Kaneko's manuscripts suddenly increased. Not only poetry magazines like *Poetics (Shigaku), Historic Course*, and *Modern Poetry*, but also general magazines and daily newspapers like *Tanka, Group (Gunzō), Literary World (Bungakkai)*, and *Japan Economic News (Nihon keizai shimbun)* wanted Kaneko's contributions. Kaneko wrote for them about his own poems, his memories of deceased poets, and his love for poetry.

In 1959, Kaneko collected his miscellaneous writings from the past and published them, along with a few new essays, as *About the Japanese (Nihonjin ni tsuite)* and *About Japanese*

Art (Nihon no geijutsu ni tsuite). He had originally maintained that poetry contained in itself criticism of all things, so
that if he wrote any criticism, it would be a redundant effort of
what his poetry had already done. Nonetheless, either requested or voluntarily, he expressed his opinions against the
ugly, unpleasant traits of man, such as egoism and imitative-
ness, and about vanity, greed, prostitution, and crime. Many
passages were like aphorisms, such as the following: "I should
have just watched your face. That would have been better than
feeling tired and disappointed after I spoke."[2] And, "My point
of view probably offers you no view other than the view that it
could distort the view of the world."[3]

Kaneko's cynicism was pointed, and words in his prose, like
words in poetry, often had multiple meanings. At another
time, however, he was quite candid:

All men are equal when they come to greed, cruelty and lust. This
is regardless of their nationality. But each nationality has a different,
terribly repulsive odor. If you hear a churlish, middle-aged Frenchman wooing in a nasal voice in French Indo-China, you will surely
hate the French no matter how pro-French you are. You should see
for yourself, if you do not believe me. This is something you might
not notice even if you would go to a foreign land twenty times. For,
foreigners hide their bad side from visitors; they show it to anyone
who lives with them and rivals them in life.[4]

According to Kaneko, the Italians and the Americans are lust-
ful and bloodthirsty, the Dutch are conceited and unfriendly,
the British are too proud and hypocritical, the Malaysians are
lazy and capricious, and the Japanese are no different from any
of them.[5] He added:

The human is no different from eels, shellfish, or seals. . . . Can-
nibalism, which had been known in both the East and the West, has
been condoned by reasoning that cannibals are not human, that they
are beasts. But, is it not that man simply has not established it as a
habit? . . . If we have no choice but to form that habit, we will be
routinely eating. . . . We have no value other than being food.[6]

About Japanese Art was in a similar vein. Abundantly em-
ploying aphorisms, it unhinged the reader who was accustomed to reading others' scholarly, systematic critiques.
Kaneko surprised unguarded critics by his bluntness and
poured the cold water of cynicism on them.

Art! just a useless trick man has learned. . . . Man is surrounded by mountains of products of the intellect and thinks he is enriched. He is very wrong; he is fundamentally as poor as before. . . . A rocket or a helicopter does not add anything to man's resources. . . . Art cannot, either. Art has created man's shadows on an imaginary stage; it has never enriched man.[7]

Kaneko insisted that man cannot be so ambitious as to live purely, because the living and the "ghosts" are no longer distinguishable in this world. Having reached the height of *Inhumanity*, Kaneko saw "art" to be the deceptive ecstasy that "artists" feel when they pull the nonliving out of life and rearrange it in such a way as to write "a history of art" to their advantage. If "art" has any function for man, Kaneko wrote, it only enables man to have a glimpse of something very realistic, such as "the state" that coldly lies. He continued:

Any masterpiece grows old. Art must vacate its position to the young. If a work does not become stale, it is clear indication that our times have become debilitated.[8]

Some publishers hoped to gather all these writings and compile Kaneko's complete works. The country's economy had begun a steady upward turn, and publishing was one of the profitable businesses. It is still customary for publishers in Japan to put out what they call *zenshū*, or "complete works," of individual writers even while the authors are alive. Some popular writers have their "complete works" published in their thirties or so and they repeat the same feat in less than a decade. To some, publishing their "complete works" means to register their names as established writers in the world of letters, regardless of their worth. To others, the *zenshū* is a way to secure a steady income, provided its sales are good. In July 1960 the Yuriika Co., the publisher of the journal *Eureka*, published the first volume of *The Complete Works of Kaneko Mitsuharu (Kaneko Mitsuharu zenshū)*. Unfortunately, however, the Yuriika Co. had to abandon the project due to the editor-owner's death. Kaneko's first *zenshū* was completed later in five volumes, sporadically published by another firm, Shōshinsha.

The journal *Eureka* ceased publication, too. There were, however, a great number of poetry journals which had been started in past years. In 1958 alone, *Imagination (Sōzō)*,

Metaphysics (Metafijikku-shi), and *White Whale (Hakugei)* had been launched to join the group of "large," as distinguished from "little," magazines. In the following year *Spear (Mori)*, *Poetic System (Shi soshiki)*, *Modern Poetry Notes (Gendaishi techō)*, *Infinity (Mugen)*, and others had been launched into the already very crowded sea of periodicals specializing in modern poetry. While all these were quite active, they were, in a sense, like feudal lords, self-important and content, on more or less the same political, cultural, and financial bases as in medieval Japan. The exception was *Infinity*, which, edited by Kusano and Murano Shirō (1901-   ) was the most prestigious and financially stable.

The period of the *Wasteland* had passed after its group members had been criticized as "Missionaries of an Educationist Sect [*keimō kyōkai no shito*] who, funded by the modern poetry school in Europe (supported ideologically by European poetry), unnecessarily spread (in postwar Japan) the venom called 'uneasiness' and contributed to colonization of Japanese poetry."[9] The critic contended that post-World War II Japan was not exactly in the same spiritual and literary condition as post-World War I Europe had been and yet the Japanese Wasteland poets did not have their own direction. The poets, including Ōoka Makoto (1931-   ), Kiyooka Takayuki (1922-   ), and Iijima Kōichi (1930-   ), responded and announced that they would formulate a much-needed new poetic theory through the actual writing of poems. Then they launched a magazine called the *Alligator (Wani)*. Their intention to present in their poetry "an antithesis to what postwar Japan had been" led them into surrealism. Whether the poet is ideologically on the right or the left was no longer important. It was flashing imagery and four-dimensional perspective which were considered important. To borrow the title of an essay by one of the leading members of the group, Ōoka, their effort was "an attempt at giving a form to the question mark."[10] Their works were, on the whole, difficult as well as different; some offered only superficial freshness in form.

Kaneko continued to be original. He was fundamentally a rebel, a man who liked "opposition," or "a seal facing the other way." In 1962, he published a book of verse, calling it *The Song like a Fart (He no yō na uta)*, and presented it—something light, smelly, and useless—to the reader, who thought that he had moved from lyricism, Symbolism, Dadaism, and the like up to surrealism. It must be noted that this was not the first time that Kaneko treated such subjects as farts. Like Baudelaire, he had treated the repulsive, such as rotting bodies. He had written about feces and a lonely prostitute urinating into her cooking basin. He had sung about excrement, expounding that to be perfectly in love was to be the lover's excrement. For Kaneko, poetry was neither an elegant game of words nor an exercise of lofty thoughts, but his life, which contained the ugly, dirty, and repulsive as well as beauty and truth. He disliked intellectual poems, the products of the mind, as much as hypocrisy and vanity, and teased both the reader who sought popularity and the critics who generated fame. *The Song like a Fart* was, like his other works, a warning for those who lacked the Self, and who thought that poetry must be beautiful and the poet divinely eternal. In a poem called "Appraisal" (*"Ge"*), Kaneko wrote:

Appraisal

Never produce a work
That might move others.
That's not the job of artists,
At least, good artists.

Good artists are those who,
Unrecognized by anyone,
Write something equal to trash
And fall into oblivion.

I am moved by those.
Good works are not
Related to culture.
They belong to the artists.

Imitation and plagiarism,
Poor quality is all right,
But never make the blunder
Of being uncovered posthumously.[11]

To this poem Kaneko added a footnote, which stated that he pitied such poets as Nakahara Chūya (1907-1937) and Miyazawa because their works were uncovered after their death and they became famous posthumously. The Japanese title "*Ge*" – Sanskrit, "Gāthā" – meant a poem to be chanted by believers in praise of Buddha's virtue and accomplishments. Kaneko's "*Ge*," though neatly arranged in four four-line stanzas, was quite prosaic. "Appraisal" was something to be thrown at, rather than to be chanted by, readers, critics, and the world.

The rest of the poems in *The Song like a Fart* were similar to "Appraisal" in form and tone. While some were sarcastic, others were paradoxical. They were Kaneko's antitheses, so to speak, to the contemporary Japanese "surrealistic" poems, if the latter were meant to be antitheses to the "postwar" Japanese poems.

In January 1963 Kaneko published an essay on his dreams.[12] When he was twenty-three or twenty-four, Kaneko wrote, he had a dream that he killed his friends and senior poets in a most violent manner. He named Momota, Fukushi, Satō Sōnosuke, and others as victims of murder in his dream. He then challenged the reader, asking if any young surrealist poets could dream of surpassing past achievements by killing the elder poets like Kusano and himself. His most recent dream, presumably the 1963 New Year's Day dream, was a composite of two little-known Japanese stories which were recorded in the early modern period. In one story, a skilled craftsman carved a wooden doll modeled after his dead love, and then the doll acquired life and became a prostitute for him, a story having a similarity to Kōda Rohan's (1867-1947) well-known novel *The Elegant Buddha (Fūryūbutsu)*. The other story was one in which the thousand-handed Goddess of Mercy rented a hand to an armless prostitute, a story resembling Kawabata's short story "One Arm" ("*Kataude*"). In his dream Kaneko played the *samisen* for his love, whose head had been replaced by a bamboo stick. With Kaneko's tune on the *samisen*, the bamboo stick turned into a toothpick and flew away in the sky until it disappeared in a golden altar. Published in a leading poetry magazine, *Modern Poetry Notes*, this was a curious essay. What Kaneko intended was, perhaps, a reiteration of the last stanza of "Appraisal," quoted earlier:

> Imitation and plagiarism,
> Poor quality is all right,

But never make the blunder
Of being uncovered posthumously.

Evidently, Kaneko was concerned with the contemporary phenomenon in which journalistic popularity was equated with literary value; he was irritated by the flattery he had been shown in the recent past. It must be remembered also that Kaneko was still living with his "love," Ōkōchi Reiko. Kaneko gave "life" to his love, who was reportedly contemplating suicide. His family was vigorously opposed to his conduct, and his "friends" pretended that they were oblivious to the affair. The world was full of hypocrisy. But what in the world would fame do for him, let alone reputation? He lived with a woman who let him play the *samisen*, so he put poems to the music, if only for a moment. Kaneko was sixty-seven years old, with a burning desire to live the rest of his life to its fullest. His sister Sute died. As for Michiyo, she was still bedridden. In the same year, 1963, Ken married. Kaneko's complete works were slowly being published. In June 1964 he became a grandfather.

Kaneko felt that he was rejuvenated: from this time to his death in June 1975, there was hardly a single month in which he did not publish something. He wrote, especially in prose, which had a wider market, about his granddaughter, his old friends, love, the emperor, and the Japanese. He also wrote about *ukiyoe*, eroticism, pornography, obscenity, and the Japanese.

One of the journals through which Kaneko published these works was *The Greenling (Ainame)*, a bimonthly which his admirers launched in August 1964 with Kaneko as its "honorary" member. Indeed, no fewer than ten young poets and poetesses had formed a group, each visiting the Kaneko house at Kichijōji, and all professing Kaneko to be their mentor. These aspiring poets asked Kaneko for comments on their published works or recommendation for the manuscripts they hoped to publish. Kaneko helped these people: he even rendered financial assistance to some of them by donating money or his calligraphy for them to sell. Kaneko would write good reviews for these people, because he knew that their work needed support.[13] *Ainame*, the Japanese title of this group magazine that Kaneko named, could also have meant "licking

each other" or "mutually supporting." *The Greenling* or
Ainame published thirty respectable issues before its cessation in February 1970.

Those who admired Kaneko's solitary pursuit of beauty, the
desperate love for Michiyo, the wandering in Southeast Asia
and Europe, and his "poems of resistance" did not esteem his
activities in this period. Some frowned upon his associations
with young poetesses, while others openly expressed their
disappointment with Kaneko's simplistic poems singing for
and about his granddaughter. Many were also critical of
Kaneko's "confessions" which a journalist by the name of
Sakurai Shigeto edited and published.

The Poems for Wakaba (*Wakaba no uta*) of July 1967 was the
collection of Kaneko's poems about and for his granddaughter
Wakaba. The title of the book could also have meant "poems
like *Wakaba* or a young leaf," which may sound more appropriate for the poet's "planning to make a fresh start." For him,
"a fresh start" meant an invigorated consciousness of his journey toward his end. He knew that his *Inhumanity* was not
really understood by anyone, and he was aware of the contrast
of his old age to the young leaf. He was able to see his own
death with detachment and humor. A poem entitled "A
Monkey" ("*Saru*") read:

A Monkey

Wakaba does not say "*saru*"
She babbles "Monkey."
The problem: due to the training
Of her father who teaches English.

Wakaba, by the time you grow up
What will Japan have become?
Will she still, like a monkey,
Be imitating the West?

More important question:
Wakaba, will you be happy?
Will you not have worries
That you cannot tell your parents?

Wakaba, even dead if I could hear you cry,
I wouldn't be able to offer you comfort,

No longer can I show you monkey walk,
Scratching my hip and head.[14]

One of the projects Kaneko had engaged in during those years was to write a series of poems on the ever-popular theme of love. He published these poems in different journals at different times. As he did so, he numbered them until he accumulated sixty-nine such pieces. He was cognizant of the fact that a young man by the name of Tanikawa Shun'tarō (1931-   ) had published, with Miyoshi's backing, his poems under such unusual titles as *The 21* and *The Graffito 99 (Rakushu 99)*. Tanikawa's works were observant, eloquent and witty with a touch of social criticism and they were well received by the general public. Kaneko published all sixty-nine of his poems on love as *Love 69 (Aijō 69)* in October 1968. In his case, "sixty-nine" connoted a certain sexual posture of lovers, presumably a perfect, eternal unity of two. It also connoted the author's records of love for sixty-nine years.

At sixty-nine, love and death were one. For, of the sixty-nine audacious poems, number nineteen was:

Love 19

Not my poems nor my essays
But it is my skull
That I want to leave with the world
As proof that I lived.

But the skull, so indistinguishable
Even between man's and woman's
Missing lips, too
If one wants to kiss it.

Suppose we are put
In the love seat of a double coffin
If it is in 69 position
We won't complain to have us rearranged.[15]

Kaneko wrote prolifically. In addition to *The Poems for Wakaba, Love 69,* and numerous articles, he published a book called *The IL* in May 1965; a two-volume translation of a Japanese historical document between August 1965 and January 1966; *A History of Despair (Zetsubō no seishin shi)* in

September 1965; *The Tragedy of the Japanese (Nihonjin no higeki)* in February 1967; a translation of Arthur Rimbaud's poems in July 1967; and *Cruelty and Inhumanity (Zankoku to hijō)* in June 1968. In March 1968, he had dissolved his relationship with Ōkōchi Reiko. Evidently, Kaneko was overworking. He suffered from a stroke in May 1969, and stayed in the hospital for two months.

Kaneko's works in this period can be characterized as a summation of his past work or even a repetition of his earlier thoughts. For example, *The IL* could be compared to *The Song of the Devil's Son* of 1949 and *The Tragedy of Man* of 1952. In the 1949 work, the devil's son, resembling Christ, was sneered at by the poor, deaf, and invalid neighbors; he was also the very image of the wandering poet. In *The Tragedy of Man*, a visitor to postwar Japan, who reminded the reader of the devil's son, was humiliated by the newspapermen. In either case criticism of any religion was not the purpose of the poem. Kaneko wanted to examine his fellow men and, as a necessary step, traced man's heart and soul to the inevitable source.

Kiyooka wrote a commentary for *The IL* and defined the book to be "the consummation of the Kaneko poetry pierced by the existential pain of the old man; the artistic sublimity which is one-dimensional and yet multi-dimensional, unrealistic and yet based on the present times."[16] In *The IL*, Kaneko pursues IL in order to disclose his anonymity, just as he followed the devil and the ghost to reveal their identity. In the first of the three parts, called "IL," IL is an impotent, limp wanderer who lacks a valid passport to any country in the world. But, later, he appears in the guise of Kaneko's old friend, who is transformed into a French missionary named Goodlaben.

> Monsieur Goodlaben,
> I believe you now
> That you are closer to God.
>
> For you are ninety
> Having nothing to do
> But to wait for His call.
>
> I bet you will put on wings,
> Once you are called,

> And fly faster than a rocket,
> Even though God is not there.
>
> Monsieur Goodlaben,
> Your beard like tobacco powder
> Covering your cheeks,
> You show less remorse than God.
>
> Your lips were only
> For touching the hem of His robe;
> Your penis never having been used.
>
> How about using it now
> As a candle in the darkness
> To find God's whereabouts
> In the corner of heaven?[17]

The world of *The IL* is barren, trapping its inhabitants, including the aged poet, in a sorry condition forever. Neither in the second part, "Fern" ("*Shida*"), which could be taken as a symbol of the woman, nor in the third part, "Scorpion's Path" ("*Sasori no michi*"), which is considered a metaphor for sperm's passage or the poet's wandering into the origin of man, is there salvation for man. There is only despair. *The IL* is a colorful variation of the theme Kaneko had presented in the earlier works.

In *A History of Despair* Kaneko further expressed his deepening sense of disappointment with man. Pointing out that vanity is the very thing that drives conscientious men to despair, he argued that vanity was generated by the social and moral conditions of the country that were intent only on imitating Western life-style and idiosyncrasies. The expression of the author's despair was his way of informing the Japanese of the loss of identity or spiritual "blank" being created in the country. The book contained depictions of the author's own "despair" – always writing in poverty against the popular trends of the times, against the masses of "seals" – and revealed details in his life, including the real names of the people who were involved in various incidents that he had written about previously. Kaneko concluded *A History of Despair* with the following proposition:

I propose here that we should despair . . . In other words, I don't want you to be deceived by the present prosperity of Japan.

Study the Japanese close to you and uncover the source of despair
in both our past and present. Examine the root of despair and cast off
the sweet dreams about our future so as to reduce possible disappointment.
Only in despair can you obtain a correct vision. . . .[18]

The Tragedy of the Japanese of 1967 was Kaneko's attempt
at locating "the root of despair" in the lives of ancient
Japanese. In order to do so, he made an extensive use of his
knowledge of Chinese and Japanese classics that he had read
in his earlier days, the kind of documents that ordinary histo-
rians might not use in writing books. For example, he quoted
the conduct code of a Hōjō family to explain how inhuman the
relationship was between the ruling warriors and their subor-
dinates. He also referred to criminal records to reveal injustice. He introduced rare documents, *The Commoners' Bag*
(Chōnin-bukuro) and *The Farmers' Bag (Hyakushō-bukuro)*,
which clearly exposed the irrational social hierarchy and the
suffering of townsmen and peasants. He used old texts on
ethics to substantiate his argument that Japanese women were
miserable, many of whom were bound to the family or to the
licensed quarters. Overall, *The Tragedy of the Japanese* was a
substantial discourse on what he had earlier depicted in "The
Song of Loneliness." Nothing was more tragic and made him
feel more lonely, Kaneko reiterated, than the state of man
chiming in with others' views. *The Tragedy of the Japanese*
was another warning for the Japanese who undiscriminatingly
followed Chinese sages, village headmen, emperors, Western
thinkers, communism, militarists, Allied Occupation Forces,
"democracy," Americans, and talkative neighbors.

On New Year's Day 1968, as in the previous years, Kaneko
was asked by the *Book News (Tosho shimbun)*, a weekly literary review, to express his New Year's Day thoughts. He commented on the so-called "poetry boom" as evidenced by the
innumerable deluxe publications of poetry, and concluded
that the "boom," artificially created by publishers, had not really produced good poems.[19] He recognized little value in the
contents of the poetry collections extravagantly bound and ex-
pensively priced. Not long ago, he had offered the following
advice to a leading poet, Tamura:

Tamura Ryūichi is a good poet—so good that I feel like patting him on the back for encouragement. But, Tamura, to be really good, you must break off with every one of those who come to pat you. I broke off with them when I was young, so I can use abusive language now.[20]

It is certain that, while publishing prolifically, Kaneko read contemporary works not only extensively but carefully. Unlike some other Japanese writers, who became increasingly inactive toward the end of their careers, Kaneko continued to be assiduous. To the above criticism that involved Tamura, Kaneko had added a consolation:.

By nature I don't praise poetry. If I had praised it, I must have been trying to be diplomatic with society, while neglecting my Self. I was critical of Hagiwara, while he was living; I was scornful of Takamura, when he was alive. Both Muroo and Satō Sōnosuke were angry with me before they died. I criticized them, because I knew that they were capable of creating better works: I had fully recognized their goodness. However, no one understood me.[21]

At that time, the magazine *Greenling* continued, and so did many others. Still, more poetry magazines appeared and many disappeared. Some of them had unusual titles, such as *Oil Drum (Doramukan)*, *Violent 'Run (Bōsō)*, *Doomed Territory (Kyōku)*, *Thud (Doin)*, *Screech (Gyā)*, and *Bad Mark (Batten)*. These titles were, by and large, indicative of the contents. The fact was that there had appeared a new generation, poets younger than Tamura, Ōoka, Kiyooka, or Tanikawa. These younger poets, born after World War II, apparently regarded poetry not as a perfected entity, but as something incomplete and moving. Their language was raw and their imagery coarse. Some works were dynamic, but many were incoherent. There were works which might be classed as surrealist or existentialist, while there were other works dealing with sex or homosexuality. Kaneko was already a grandparent, so to speak, of these younger poets.

Kaneko was often invited by the contributors to *Greenling* to a restaurant or some such place and was asked his opinions on contemporary poetry. He was also asked to participate in public lectures. At no time, however, did he act as a dean: he

never posed as an authoritative critic. Unlike many famous
poets, Kaneko did not build a tower of theories; nor did he
often discuss poetics. He totally disliked being pedantic and
chose to remain a mere poet, a man of his own words from his
own heart. The discriminating reader recognized that, at the
basis of Kaneko's poetry, there was an inpenetrable core. It
was this hard core, together with his skull, that caused Kaneko
to stand firmly in the midst of different currents of poetry and
many groups of poets. Kaneko occupied an immovable position in the world of poetry due to the solidity of his Self, even
though he did not build a grandiose sand castle of poetics. His
career was living proof that the main trend might really be
insubstantial and ephemeral, and the secondary might well be
first-rate; the ugly, truthful; and opposition, righteous.

In 1968, Kaneko published a collection of essays that he had
written for various periodicals in past years, called *Cruelty
and Inhumanity*. The topics of the essays varied from the
U.S.-Japan Security Pact and the Japanese Constitution to
memories of his trips abroad, his acquaintances, and his boyhood. In dealing with political issues, however, Kaneko, as in
his other essays and poems, did not discuss politics. For him,
the political right and the political left were as much the same
as love and death. Individuals' attitudes toward the issues
were what mattered. In the essay on the U.S.-Japan Security
Pact, which upset the entire nation and drove fanatics like
Mishima to madness during the 1960s, Kaneko wrote about
the people who did not pursue the issues to completion and
who were content with a superficial freedom of speech and
material prosperity represented by the so-called "leisure
boom."[22] He referred to the recent incident in which the publisher of the *Public Review* was assassinated by a right-wing
terrorist, and compared contemporary journalists, novelists,
and poets to those who blindly followed the military government during the war. It was intolerable for Kaneko to witness
the *Public Review*, the journal which published many of his
"poems of resistance," being terrorized.

Other essays in *Cruelty and Inhumanity* depicted human
misery resulting from excessive power, desires, ignorance,
and lack of an individual's Self. Kaneko revealed wartime ab-
surdities like keeping the hair of women's private parts as a
bullet-proof talisman, and reminded the reader how stupid

man could be in the face of war and the draft system. Some critics labeled this and other writings that directly dealt with "the repulsive" as Kaneko's "exposure mania." For Kaneko, ugliness was as truthful as beauty, and exposing filth was a way to reach truth from "the other way." Pretending to be bad, Kaneko challenged man, who only pretended to be good. His "indecency" was a bitter criticism of hypocrisy and of materialistic, "decent" life, which the Japanese were enjoying at that time. Many younger poets were "decent"; some were indeed well-to-do. Kaneko reminisced with warmth and affection about his old friends who died without having enjoyed a "decent" life. He felt that life was cruel, for many "indecent" writers died before their works were justly appreciated.

The Short Literary Essays by Kaneko Mitsuharu (Kaneko Mitsuharu bungakuteki dansō) was, despite its title, Kaneko's fond recollections of the people with whom he associated, accompanied by his introductions and forewords to books of poetry by other poets. He published it at the end of 1969, a year after Kawabata received the first Nobel Prize for Literature in Japan. Of all men, whether miserable or triumphant, feeling lonely or not, Kaneko had a special favorable prejudice toward poets. For example, his essay called "Hoizumi Yoshisuke"—possibly the only record of this obscure writer—registered vividly, and with deep affection, the Hoizumi brothers, who, half a century earlier, had introduced Kaneko to literature before they died of tuberculosis. Kaneko's depiction of the brothers' different attitude to geisha was a splendid characterization of the unfortunate Hoizumi. It was with them that Kaneko wrote his first poem:

> Of course I am opposed
> To patriotism or humanity.
> I am opposed to government
> The world of writers and artists.
>
> If asked what I was born for
> My answer Is: "To oppose."
> I in the east
> Longing for the west.
>
> Clothes reversed, shoes on the wrong feet
> Pants twisted, I mount a horse backward
> . . .

In this *Short Literary Essays*, Kaneko named Hagiwara, Muroo, Okamoto, and a few others as the poets who gave him literary nourishment. But he added that these poets might not do the same to the reader, and when he wrote about his poems, he warned that he and the reader were not the same so that his essay on his poems might not hold the same meaning for everyone. Further, in "Poetry and I" ("*Watakushi to shi*"), he proclaimed that he did not belong to the lineage of past poets; that he was not really a poet. With a certain bitterness wrapped in cynicism he concluded that his poetry was merely to satisfy his ego; that he would not be understood according to the conventional standards.[23]

Yet Kaneko was sought after. He was asked to participate in round-table discussions on all sorts of subjects by magazines and newspapers of all kinds. He was frequently requested by broadcasting firms to appear on television. He accepted the invitations and went out, wearing Japanese clothes rather than the contemporary suit and tie. Kaneko's "weathered" dandyism no longer consisted of the black formal attire and silk hat that he had worn in London and Paris. Like the nineteenth-century Japanese dilettante writers who turned their back on the world, he put on a kimono untidily and dragged worn-out clogs to go to fashionable places of appointment. Besides, he usually walked the distance that other people would have traveled by taxi or bus. He was generally healthy, except that he was hard of hearing.

In November 1969, the *Public Review*, still one of the most prestigious monthlies even after the editor had been assassinated, began serializing Kaneko's prose work under a curious title. Called "A Skull"("*Dokuro-hai*"), it was a story of his visits to Shanghai and its surrounding area. In this, however, the poet beautifully blurred the borderline between fact and fantasy, between seriousness and mockery. The result was autobiographical fiction, so to speak, in which Kaneko showed, in the record of travels, flashes of his solid Self in contrast to the vanity of man. He asserted that, if his poems were lost, his skull would remain. Later published as a book, "A Skull" reminded the reader of his earlier poem on love.

> Not my poems nor my essays
> But it is my skull

That I want to leave with the world
As proof that I lived.

Japan was quickly surpassing England, France, and West
Germany in terms of gross national product. For Japan the on-
going war in Vietnam was like a fire on the other side of a
river. The country prospered. The people were satisfied possessing "the three C's," namely, color television, cooler (air-
conditioner), and a car. Materialism and egotism dominated;
philosophy and thought were secondary. Some worried
educationalists made puns on the wartime national slogan and
warned about "One Hundred Million Japanese Idiot-ization"
(*"Ichioku sōhakuchi"*). They blamed television, which was in
almost all households, equalizing the taste, language, and
thought of the people from the one end of the country to the
other. In addition to television, there were daily papers of
similar kinds, monthly journals on many popular subjects, and
numerous weeklies which were sold, some by the millions, at
every station of the minutely woven network of surface, un-
derground, and elevated railways. The entire nation was one
huge journalistic melting pot. Just then, the novelist Mishima,
deploring the lack of spirituality and the constitutional right to
rearm, killed himself by *seppuku*, in the traditional samurai
fashion. The public was stunned, but soon looked for more
excitement and stimuli. For such masses Kaneko was an interesting, provocative old man, skilled specially in "erotic"
talk. They continued to demand Kaneko's contributions and
appearances. The Japan Pro Chorus made tunes for his poems
and sang them at concerts. At the twenty-sixth anniversary
of the end of the Pacific War *The Asahi*, one of the nation's
leading papers, asked Kaneko's opinions about the present
condition of Japan. Kaneko's answer, published on August 10,
1971, was somber: he noted man's untrustworthiness and
warned the public that contemporary pacifists would turn to
fascists once a war occurred in Japan.

In June 1971, Kaneko had published two books, *New Miscellaneous Notes (Shin zatsuji hishin)* and *A Biography of the
Inhuman (Nimpinin den)*. The former was a record of his talks
on such subjects as his study of Chinese literature, his opinion
on rhetoric and poetry, his memories of the end of the Pacific
War, his boyhood, and his taste for food. The latter was the

story of Kaneko, which was edited by Sakurai Shigeto, the journalist associated with the *Greenling*. The book manifested the skills of Sakurai as an editor. After the completion of *Inhumanity* in 1955 Kaneko was like a lone wolf, rather than a hermit, in the jungle of journalism.

In September of the same year he published yet another book, *A Record of Transfiguration (Fūryū shikai ki)*, a novel, containing more than ten poems which he had published in the 1950s. He posed as a writer of the *kibyōshi*, or "the yellow-covered light literature book," which was popular in the early nineteenth century, and narrated a love story of an old married man and a young blind girl against the background of postwar Japan. The subject matter and style of this "novel" had been explored by Kaneko in his earlier works, and the image of the girl overlapped those of "the pom-pom girl" and the mysterious beauty in Batu Pahat.

A clue to this "novel" lay in its unusual title, which meant something like "an amorous record of a hermit's transfiguration after reaching an understanding of the truth."[24] Kaneko and Yokomitsu had recognized each other as hermits at Kichijōji Station, and Yokomitsu had died in adversity. Takamura, who had lived his postwar years like a hermit in the mountains, had also died. Surely, Kaneko too. . . . The book was an answer to the question: what should a poet become transformed into? It is into nothingness, for the word *"shikai"* in the title meant "melting or dispersing of the body." Man should not leave anything in this world, once he has attained the truth. The old man in the book seemed to have reached *satori*, the understanding of man and the world, so he would melt and disperse. *A Record of Transfiguration*, containing the facts of Kaneko's life behind the mist of poetic truth, was also his farewell to Ōkōchi Reiko and the other women in his life. He was a poet who, even in his most autobiographical book, *The Poet*, did not carelessly show his naked Self. His poetry told his life, and vice versa.

On March 11, 1972, Kaneko was awarded the Education Minister's Prize of 100,000 yen for his "achieving excellence and opening up a new realm of art during the past year."[25] When news of the award reached the Kaneko home, Kaneko was not there and Ken arranged the acceptance of the prize.[26] Kaneko did not attend the ceremony to receive it. It was, however, worthy of a private celebration for Kaneko that *A Record of Transfiguration* was one of the reasons for the award by the Education Minister of the country: he visited the widow of Tanizaki at Yugawara, a little far from Tokyo, and thanked the widow for the favor and understanding which the late novelist had extended to him at times of his crises. Kaneko was seventy-six years old; Tanizaki had died at seventy-nine in 1965.

That year, Kaneko started serial publication of a new work in the *Public Review*. The work, called "Sleep, Paris" (*"Nemure Pari"*), was a sequel to *A Skull*. No sooner than this was published as a book in October 1973, he published *The Perverse (Amanojaku)*, which was a collection of his miscellaneous writings for newspapers and magazines. He closed this book comparing it to an acquaintance's book which was reported to have been used page by page as toilet paper. Meanwhile, he serialized "The Gate for All Beings" (*"Shūmyō no mon"*) for the magazine *Half Serious (Omoshiro hambun)*. "The gate for all beings," denoting "the gate of universal truth," connoted a certain anatomical "gate" for all men in Kaneko's story. Set in the places where Kaneko had actually lived, the story depicted relations with various women. This work, dictated by Kaneko to Sakurai, who edited it, was boldly explicit in describing sexual acts. *The Gate for All Beings* became a book in September 1974.

The editor Sakurai one day asked Kaneko a serious question: what was Kaneko's opinion of contemporary Japanese poetry? Kaneko answered that present-day poetry looked to him like translations by learned scholars, not like poems by poets; that today's poets seemed to him either weird, self-important men or cheap scholars.[27] Indeed, many poems still treated the all-time popular subjects, such as love, loneliness, isolation, and poverty, but they were by and large products of the intellect. In many poems there were only clusters of imagery, either suggesting such subjects or not suggesting anything at all. In some poems there were only clusters of meaningless words. Poetry was an entity not attached in any way to poets' lives. A distinction lies in Kaneko's subtly personal poems, such as those included in *The Flower and an Empty Bottle (Hana to akibin)*, his last published book of verse.

Perhaps Kaneko instinctively knew that it was going to be

his last book, as he wrote a short "Personal News" ("*Kinkyō*")
for the daily paper *Asahi* on October 23, 1972, and announced
to the public that he had finished more than half of *The Flower
and an Empty Bottle*. He concluded the announcement with a
perverse remark: he deplored his poverty and wrote that he
wanted to share the good luck of Shiga Naoya (1883-1971), a
writer of a rich family who lived in luxury after having published only one long novel. Shiga, labeled "God of the Novel"
for his excellent short stories back in the 1910s, had passed
away, leaving his reputation as a great novelist intact.

In August 1973 Kaneko started to serialize a prose work
called "The West and the East" ("*Nishi higashi*"). A sequel to
Sleep, Paris, this was an enlarged version of a part of *The
Poet*, for it detailed his experience in Southeast Asia, where he
had stopped on his way back to Japan from Europe in 1931 and
1932. This work was concluded in September 1974. Also, in
1973, Kaneko had published *Stories of Love and Poetry* (*Ai to
shi monogatari*), which was actually an expanded version of
his earlier essay on others' poems that he favored.

In his last published book of poems, *The Flower and an
Empty Bottle* of September 1973, Kaneko was loquacious.
Most poems in it were long, and they showed some stylistic
resemblances to *Inhumanity*: two-line stanzas of complete or
incomplete sentences prevailed, giving the poems a continu-
ous shift of imagery. But the value of the poems lay in the
clarity of meaning, a glaring contrast to the ambiguous contemporary poems, and the power of poetry that drew the
reader to the heart of the poet. The empty bottle was at one
time a hard crystal, and at another it assumed the appearance
of a totally different object. For example, in the following
poem, called "A Short Poem B" ("*Tanshi B*"), the bottle was
not an ordinary glass product.

> If man becomes extinct
> It is God and lice who will suffer.
> If I become extinct
> It is my tongue that will suffer
> Unable to lick.
>
> My tongue licked the bottle
> Loving it from mouth to bottom;
> The bottle in return embarrassed me

> Talking nonsense all the way
> For seventy years.

> In death, my only regret will be
> That I did not have enough helium
> To blow the bottle
> And make it float
> Until it reached heaven.[28]

It might be noted that the title of this book could also be translated as "A Flower and the Empty Bottle." If the flower were beauty or poetry, the latter might be a soda bottle or the empty world. If one were a woman, the other would be the poet floating down a polluted river. If one were life or impermanence, the other would be death or permanence. In other words, the bottle could be "the gate for all beings."

Kaneko wrote a postscript to this book, saying how some people were surprised to find him still writing poems and, in his own sarcastic way, remarked that the reader was not obliged to read this book. He noted that this collection would neither refresh the reader like soda pop, nor warm him like *saké*; that it was like a muffled cry through a closed glass-door, asserting to the reader that he was still alive.[29] In one of the short poems in the book, Kaneko had written:

> Before you go, passers-by
> Place a flower
> In the old empty bottle, won't you?
> If you notice it, that is.[30]

The passers-by did not offer Kaneko a flower. The passers-by took Kaneko as an entertaining, erotic old man; they did not hear Kaneko's cry. Not only magazine editors but also photographers abused him. Cameramen took his pictures in settings like the backstage of a striptease theater, and held special Kaneko exhibits at galleries and department-store halls. Art dealers held shows of Kaneko's poetry and sketches. Television continued to request his appearance on talk shows, where he talked about striptease, pornographic painting, venereal disease, obscenity, and other topics as requested. Younger poets put him on the editorial boards of their journals. He often attended their meetings and offered help as requested.

At the beginning of 1974, Kaneko suffered from insomnia, for which he took sleeping pills. One day in March, while at a barber shop, he suffered a second stroke.

Kaneko recovered from the stroke in about two weeks, and in April he published a book called *People, Please Be Generous (Hito yo yuruyaka nare)*. The book contained about fifty brief essays, featuring the one entitled "People, Please Be Generous." He wrote that his heart was chilled, as he realized that the only way for man to avoid tragedy was for each individual to reflect on his inner life. The book also contained translations of Pushkin which were, according to Kaneko, those that he had done in Paris some fifty years before. With this, Kaneko exhausted his supply of old manuscripts to pass onto the publishers.

Kaneko's activities did not stop, however. In July 1974 he began serving as the editor of the journal *Half Serious*. At the same time, he assisted young writers to launch a journal called *Just a Moment (Isasaka)*. He must have been conscious of these journal titles, both of which were ultimately befitting to his state of mind at that time. From January to June 1974 Kaneko drew illustrations for *Half Serious*, and in July of that year he started to dictate another story to Sakurai. In January 1975 he even sang for an audience in Osaka. Meanwhile, for *Just a Moment*, he continued to write "The Six Worlds" ("*Rikudō*"), the poem which he left unfinished at his death. "The Six Worlds" was obviously an attempt to depict the world after death, filled with lively, dark desires, as in this world. Few in this world understood Kaneko anymore. He was flying in the limitless sky of other worlds.

On a talk show on April 18, 1975, Kaneko unusually argued in a strong tone against Tanikawa, the fashionable young poet of *The Graffito 99*. He remarked that Tanikawa had no real understanding of his poetry. Tanikawa then glossed over Kaneko's challenge, saying that he had "reluctantly" recognized the Kaneko poetry and understood it.[31] Kaneko in return advised Tanikawa that the poet should not recognize others; that Tanikawa should recognize himself, while writing, as the greatest poet. The half-serious talk show contained Kaneko's plea to the audience that he be forgotten after his death.

About 11:30 A.M. on June 30, 1975, Kaneko complained of a pain in his chest. It was another stroke. Before he died, he was reported to have said, "Is this it, I wonder?" His funeral was held without any reference to religion.

Michiyo had written about Kaneko's initial stroke of 1969.[32] According to her, as he was being carried away on a stretcher, he said to her, "Forgive me." Michiyo, totally upset and unable to come close to Kaneko because of her rheumatism, replied to him from her bed, "Good-bye"; then Kaneko smiled and said, "Not good-bye, but *au revoir*." Michiyo and Ken later discussed the implications of "Forgive me." She alone, Michiyo had written, knew exactly what Kaneko meant.

Notes and References

Chapter One

1. Kaneko Mitsuharu. *Kaneko Mitsuharu zenshū* (Tokyo, Chūō Kōron Sha, 1975-77), hereafter KMZ, IX, p. 196.
2. This poem, known in Japanese as *"Hantai,"* was not published until 1951, when the poet Akiyama Kiyoshi compiled one of the first anthologies of Kaneko's poems for Sōgensha, Tokyo. It is included in the "Gleanings" volume of KMZ. Conceivably, this is not the oldest extant poem by Kaneko. KMZ, V, p. 157.
3. KMZ, VI, pp. 70-71.
4. KMZ, XIII, p. 151.
5. KMZ, I, pp. 109-10.
6. Ibid., 104.
7. Ibid., 107.
8. KMZ, XII, pp. 20-22.
9. Ibid., 54-57.
10. KMZ, VI, p. 144.
11. KMZ, I, pp. 133-36.
12. Ibid., 580.
13. Ibid., 138.
14. Ibid., 155-57.
15. Ibid., 528.

Chapter Two

1. Murano Shirō, comp., *Kaneko Mitsuharu shishū* (Tokyo, 1974), pp. 30-31.
2. *Kaneko Mitsuharu zenshū* (Tokyo, Yuriika, 1960), I, pp. 197-200. Kaneko revised the poem to this form, when he included it in his first *zenshū*. The 1926 version is shorter in form, stiffer in style, and harder in content. The revised version is used here by reason of its suitability.

3. KMZ, XI, p. 160.

4. Okamoto Jun's recollection, published originally in *Yuriika*, is quoted by Satō Sōsuke, *Kaneko Mitsuharu samayoeru tamashii* (Tokyo, 1974), pp. 20-21.

5. KMZ, VII, p. 132.

Chapter Three

1. Nakano Shigeharu, "*Shi ni kansuru ni-san no dampen,*" *Roba*, No. 3 (June 1926), p. 6-7. The Japanese for these terms are *Gensōshi-ha, Kaisōshi-ha,* and *Kyōkanshi-ha*.

2. KMZ, II, pp. 8-12.

3. Ibid., 40-41.

4. Ibid., 43-44.

5. Ibid., 48-53.

6. Ibid., 53-56.

7. KMZ, XII, p. 321. Also, KMZ, IV, p. 348.

8. KMZ, XII, pp. 345-46. This passage may be compared with Nagai Kafū's (1876-1959) famous essay "*Hanabi.*" Having witnessed the rise of fascism and political injustice, Nagai announced that he was going to spend the rest of his life like a *gesakusha*, a nineteenth-century dilettante writer who detested power and lived detached from social and political issues.

9. KMZ, VIII, p. 418.

10. KMZ, VI, p. 193.

11. KMZ, XII, pp. 86-87.

12. KMZ, VI, p. 194.

13. KMZ, II, pp. 88-90.

14. Takamura wrote the poem "*Netsuke no kuni*" in 1910 and published it in the following year in *Subaru*. For an English translation, see Donald Keene, comp., *Modern Japanese Literature: an Anthology* (New York, 1956), p. 206.

15. This poem, "*Ippai no gohan,*" is accompanied by a note saying that it was composed on July 23, 1944, at the foot of Mount Fuji. KMZ, II, pp. 118-19.

16. KMZ, VI, p. 200.

17. KMZ, II, pp. 251-53.

18. For details, see Kaneko's "*Kotto-san no nyūin*" in *Tori wa su ni* (Tokyo, 1975), pp. 149-56.

Chapter Four

1. This poem is entitled "*Tokyo no haikyo ni tatte,*" which means literally, "Standing in the Ruins of Tokyo." KMZ, II, pp. 142-44.

2. KMZ, III, pp. 155-56.

3. *Kosumosu*, No. 1 (1946), p. 25. This was later given the title "*Nihonjin ni tsuite*" and was included in *About the Japanese Art.* KMZ, XI, p. 219.

4. *Kosumosu*, No. 1 (1946), p. 2.

5. Hara Masaji notes that Kaneko maintained his relationship with Ōkōchi Reiko until 1968. Satō Sōsuke writes that the poet Akiyama Kiyoshi witnessed the marriage between Kaneko and Ōkōchi. The new chronological chart in KMZ, XV, reveals more such information. The Kaneko family register, which I examined by courtesy of Nakajima Kaichirō, did indicate that Kaneko married Ōkōchi in 1958 after having divorced Michiyo in the same year. The family register also indicated that Kaneko had been entered in the Mori family record in 1958, renouncing the surname Kaneko perhaps as Michiyo's defensive measure against Ōkōchi, and that Michiyo remarried Kaneko in 1965. This means that Kaneko died Mori Yasukazu. There is also Ōkōchi's memoir which, though edited heavily by a journalist, corroborates these facts. Cf. Hara Masaji, comp., "*Kaneko Mitsuharu nempu*," *Gendaishi techō* (September, 1975), p. 124. Satō Sōsuke. *Kaneko Mitsuharu samayoeru tamashii* (Tokyo, 1974), p. 217. Ōkōchi Reiko. *Kaneko Mitsuharu no rabu-retā* (Tokyo, 1976).

6. KMZ, II, pp. 154-55. Three complete translations of this important poem are available elsewhere: one by this author in *Literature East and West*, 1971 and 1972 combined issue, and the others by Takagi Keiko in *Japan Quarterly*, 1976, and by Howard S. Hibbett in his *Contemporary Japanese Literature*, 1977. See Selected Bibliography.

7. Ibid., 156-57.

8. Ibid., 157-59.

9. Ibid., 160-61.

10. Ibid., 165.

11. Ibid., 272-74.

12. Ibid., 204-06.

13. Ibid., 171-72.

14. Ibid., 173.

15. Ibid., 174.

16. Ibid., 175.

17. Ibid., 177-78.

18. KMZ, III, pp. 10-11.

19. Nakajima Kaichirō, "*Kami tono taiwa*," *Gendaishi techō* (May 1965), p. 139.

20. Shutō Motozumi, *Kaneko Mitsuharu kenkyū* (Tokyo, 1970), p. 140.

21. Cited in *Meiji Taishō Shōwa shi shi* (Tokyo, 1969), p. 383.

22. Hatanaka Shigeo, *"Mori-san no koto ni furenagara,"* KMZ *geppō*, No. 6, p. 2.

23. Mori Ken, *"Shijin no hokori,"* Ainame *Kaneko Mitsuharu tsuitō-gō* (December 1975), p. 42.

24. KMZ, III, pp. 113-14.

25. Ibid., 119-20.

26. Ibid., 130-31.

27. Ibid., 134-35.

28. Ibid., 178.

29. Ibid., 193-95.

30. Okamoto Jun, *"Kaneko Mitsuharu e no tegami,"* Gendaishi (January 1955), pp. 30-35. Read especially pp. 33-35.

31. Quoted by Okamoto Jun in his *"Mōhitotsu no kao,"* Hon no techō (June 1963), p. 20. Kaneko's review, first published in *Gendaishi* in 1955, is included in KMZ, XV, pp. 490-91.

32. KMZ, III, p. 400.

33. Ibid., 236.

34. Ibid., 237. This translation is based on a revised version. It is to be noted that Kaneko sometimes revised works as he republished them. KMZ is based on the original editions.

35. KMZ, III, pp. 242-43.

36. Ibid., 308-12.

37. Ibid., 312-17.

Chapter Five

1. KMZ, VI, p. 217.

2. KMZ, XI, p. 14.

3. Ibid., 17.

4. Ibid., 19.

5. Ibid.

6. Ibid., 38.

7. Ibid., 169.

8. Ibid., 173.

9. *"Gendaishi no suitai to saiken,"* Rettō (September 1953), p. 5.

10. Ōoka Makoto wrote an essay called *"Gimonfu o sonzaisaseru kokoromi"* for *Wani* in 1960.

11. KMZ, IV, pp. 30-31.

12. KMZ, XIII, pp. 212-14.

13. Mori Ken, *"Shijin no hokori,"* p. 45.

14. KMZ, IV, pp. 256-57.

15. Ibid., 354-55.

16. Ibid., 446.

17. Ibid., 77-79.

18. KMZ, XII, p. 108.

19. KMZ, VII, p. 472.

20. Ibid., 392.

21. Ibid.

22. Ibid., 217-24.

23. KMZ, XIII, p. 20.

24. In a conversation with the poet Kiyooka Takayuki, Kaneko interpreted the word *"shikai"* used in the title. He said that he used it in a sense different from the interpretation he had given to Kiyooka. Cf. *"Kizudarake no sengo," Yuriika* (May 1972), p. 72.

25. *Asahi shimbun*, March 11, 1952.

26. This information was given to me by Nakajima Kaichirō.

27. Quoted by Kitagawa Fuyuhiko in his *"Kaneko Mitsuharu montāju," KMZ geppō*, No. 10, p. 6.

28. KMZ, V, p. 78.

29. Ibid., 94-95.

30. Ibid., 78.

31. Tanikawa Shuntarō, Ibaragi Noriko and Kaneko Mitsuharu, *"Shi ni okeru hyōgen," Gendaishi techō* (December 1975), p. 200.

32. Mori Michiyo, *"Eibetsu yo, yuruyakani," Yuriika* (May 1972), p. 85

Selected Bibliography

PRIMARY SOURCES

There are two sets of collected works of Kaneko Mitsuharu. They are:

Kaneko Mitsuharu zenshū. Tokyo: Yuriika and Shōshinsha, 1960-1970.
5v.
Kaneko Mitsuharu zenshū. Tokyo: Chūō Kōron Sha, 1975-1977. 15 v.
The former, compiled while the author was alive, is a selection. It
contains the revised version of "The Song of Wandering" ("*Hyōhaku
no uta*") and Kaneko's diary of his younger days. Each volume of this
set is accompanied by leading critics' commentaries. The latter, posthumously compiled, is more complete. It includes most poems, as
they appeared in the individual collections. It also contains Kaneko's
translations of French poems and a good selection of autobiographical works, literary essays, forewords to others' books, and individually published miscellaneous writings. At the end of each volume are
brief annotations and bibliographical details about the works. Volume
fifteen contains a comprehensive chronology updated by the compil-
ers of the collection. There is no index.

The chronologies in the above and the other works often contain
bibliographic information on not only Kaneko's books but also on his
articles published in journals and newspapers. These chronologies,
however, are apparently based on the following works, the first two of
which are by Nakajima Kaichirō:
"*Nempu*," in *Teihon Kaneko Mitsuharu zen-shishū*. Tokyo: Chikuma
Shobō, 1969, pp. 1091-1119.
"*Shōsai Kaneko Mitsuharu nempu*," *Yuriika*, IV (1972), 180-90.
HARA MASAJI, "*Kaneko Mitsuharu nempu*," *Gendaishi techō*, IIXX
(1975), 112-27. This is another useful chronology.

Single-volume collections of Kaneko's poems are numerous, and
most of them include commentaries as well as chronologies. Some
provide bibliographies. The most noteworthy is the aforementioned

Teihon Kaneko Mitsuharu zen-shishū, published by Chikuma Shobō in 1969. Beautifully printed in large type, this is a luxurious edition to own. Due to the publication date, however, the book is obviously limited in its coverage. Other representative books are:

AKIYAMA KIYOSHI, comp. *Kaneko Mitsuharu shishū*. Tokyo: Sōgensha, 1951.

YAMANOGUCHI BAKU, comp. *Kaneko Mitsuharu shishū*. Tokyo: Shinchōsha, 1952.

Gendai Nihon shijin zenshū (Zen shishū taisei, IIX). Tokyo: Sōgensha, 1954.

ANDO TSUGUO, comp. *Kaneko Mitsuharu (Nihon shijin zenshū*, XXIV). Tokyo: Shinchōsha, 1967.

NAKAJIMA KAICHIRŌ, comp. *Kaneko Mitsuharu shishū (Seishun no shishū*, XIX). Tokyo: Hakuōsha, 1968.

IBARAGI NORIKO, comp. *Kaneko Mitsuharu shishū (Sekai no shi*, ILIV). Tokyo; Yayoi Shobō, 1969.

MURANO SHIRO, comp. *Kaneko Mitsuharu shishū*. Tokyo: Ōbunsha, 1974.

Kaneko Mitsuharu shishū, with commentary by Tamura Ryūichi. Tokyo: Shichōsha, 1975.

TRANSLATIONS

A list of translations of Kaneko's poems is to be found in *Modern Japanese Literature in Western Translations: A Bibliography*, compiled by the International House of Japan Library in 1972. This *Bibliography* indicates, for example, that the *Penguin Book of Japanese Verse* included in 1964 three poems by Kaneko. More recent translations, not included in the above, are:

MORITA, JAMES R., tr. "Poems of Kaneko Mitsuharu," *Literature East and West*, XV, No. 4; XVI, No. 1; XVI, No. 2 (December 1971 and March and June 1972) combined issue, pp. 803-15.

TAKAGI KEIKO, tr. "Poems of Kaneko Mitsuharu," *Japan Quarterly*, XXIII (1976), 274-83.

HIBBETT, HOWARD S., and MORITA, JAMES R., tr. "Three poems." *Contemporary Japanese Literature*, comp. by Howard S. Hibbett. New York: Knopf, 1977, pp. 310-17.

SECONDARY SOURCES

An excellent English guide to Japanese poetry is Thomas Rimer and Robert Morrell's *Guide to Japanese Poetry*, published by G. K. Hall and Co. in 1975. It gives a good overview of the development of poetry in Japan as well as critical commentaries on English works on

Japanese poetry. Works deserving a separate mention include: Ueda Makoto's "Japanese Literature Since World War II," in *The Literary Review*, Autumn, 1962; Donald Keene's "Modern Japanese Poetry," in his *Landscapes and Portraits* (Tokyo, 1971); and Atsumi Ikuko's "New Epics of Cultural Convergence," in *Japan Interpreter*, XI, no. 3.

Japanese sources are innumerable. Virtually all books on Japanese literature devote some pages to modern Japanese poetry. Of these, those found to have good coverage of poetry are:

Nihon bungaku no rekishi. Tokyo: Kadokawa Shoten, 1968. 12 v.

MIYOSHI YUKIO and TAKEMORI TENYŪ, comp. *Kindai bungaku*. Tokyo: Yūhikaku, 1967-77. 10 v.

There are a great number of Japanese books concentrating on modern Japanese poetry. Furukawa Kiyohiko's *"Kindaishi sankō bunken"* in Vol. 23 of *Kindai bungaku kanshō kōza* (Tokyo: Kadokawa Shoten, 1962), and the selected bibliographies in Seki Ryōichi's *Kindaishi* (Tokyo: Yūseido, 1967), are still useful guides to works on modern Japanese poetry. Seki's guide is revised in his *Kindaishi no keitai to seiritsu*, (Tokyo: Kyōiku Shuppan Center, 1976). Peculiarly, a rather old work, Hinatsu Kōnosuke's *Meiji Taishō shi shi*, published by Sōgensha, Tokyo, in three volumes in 1948, is unsurpassed by any book yet. It is by far the most comprehensive book on the history of modern Japanese poetry. In addition, the following three, though varied in the arrangement, contain contributions by foremost scholars and are very illuminating:

Meiji Taishō Shōwa shi shi (*Gendaishi kanshō kōza*, XII). Tokyo: Kadokawa Shoten, 1968-69. 12 v.

Gendai shiron taikei. Tokyo: Shichōsha, 1965-67. 6 v.

Kōza Nihon gendaishi shi. Tokyo: Yūbun Shoin, 1973. 4 v.

Most commercial journals of Japanese literature, such as *Kokubungaku kaishaku to kyōzai no kenkyū* and *Kokubungaku kaishaku to kanshō*, have published special numbers devoted to the study of modern Japanese poetry. Identified by subtitles, such as *Kindaishi no rekishi* and *Kindaishi kara gendaishi e* on both cover and spine of the journals, all of these special numbers are extremely useful. Poetry journals, while they are primary sources, often publish serious studies of modern Japanese poetry. Of numerous such journals, *Gendaishi techō*, *Shigaku*, and *Yuriika* cannot be overlooked. The June 1963 issue of *Hon no techō* and the January 1968 issue of *Chikyū* exclusively discuss Kaneko and his works. Little magazines like *Ainame*, *Jikan*, and *Yonjigen* are also important. Memorial issues for Kaneko, especially of reputable journals, are very useful. Regrettably, there is still no index to the articles in these journals.

For studies exclusively on Kaneko, bibliographies are available. The most recent one is Volume II of *Nihon bungaku kenkyū bunken yōran* (Tokyo: Nichigai Associates, 1977), which lists the Japanese works on Kaneko published between 1965 and 1974. Of the works retrievable through the above, essays by such poets as Kiyooka Takayuki, Ōoka Makoto, Iijima Kōichi, Tamura Ryūichi, and Akiyama Kiyoshi cannot be ignored. These poets are excellent critics as well.

The aforementioned chronologies by Nakajima and Hara are both followed by bibliographies. Nakajima classifies works by types, such as monographs and newspaper articles, whereas Hara arranges them all in straight chronological order from 1926 to 1975. Some noteworthy single-volume studies of Kaneko are:

SHUTŌ MOTOZUMI. *Kaneko Mitsuharu kenkyū*. Tokyo: Shimbisha, 1970.

HORIKI MASAMICHI. *Shiteki Kaneko Mitsuharu ron*. Tokyo: Rironsha, 1972.

SHIMAOKA AKIRA. *Kaneko Mitsuharu ron*. Tokyo: Satsuki Shobō, 1973.

While the above works are quite scholarly, the following books are rather personal in nature, informing of aspects of Kaneko's life.

SATŌ SŌSUKE. *Kaneko Mitsuharu seishun no ki*. Tokyo: Shin Jimbutsu Ōraisha, 1972.

———. *Kaneko Mitsuharu samayoeru tamashii*. Tokyo: Shin Jimbutsu Ōraisha, 1974.

ŌKOCHI REIKO. *Kaneko Mitsuharu no rabu-retā*. Tokyo: Peppu Shuppan, 1976.

There are also books that contain records of interviews with Kaneko by various journalists. Useful are:

KAIKŌ KEN. *Hito to sono sekai*. Tokyo: Kawade Shobō Shinsha, 1970.

UCHIMURA GŌZŌ. *Dokuhaku no kōsaku*. Tokyo: Tōjusha, 1971.

In addition to all these, there are numerous books on Japanese poetry containing analyses and commentaries of Kaneko's poems. While some of these are mere annotations on terminology, others are critical studies of poetry. Some annotations are very helpful, and most commentaries are illuminating. Considered representative are:

Ono Tōzaburō. "*Kaneko Mitsuharu hen*," *Gendaishi kanshō, Shōwa-ki*. Tokyo: Daini Shobō, 1951.

ITŌ SHINKICHI. *Kaneko Mitsuharu*," *Gendaishi no kanshō*. Tokyo: Shinchōsha, 1954.

YOSHIDA SEIICHI. "*Tōdai*," *Nihon kindaishi kanshō, Shōwa-hen*. Tokyo: Shinchōsha, 1954.

MURANO SHIRŌ. "*Kaneko Mitsuharu no shi*," *Gendaishi dokuhon*. Tokyo: Kawade Shobō, 1955.

ONCHI TERUTAKE. "*Kaneko Mitsuharu*," *Gendaishi no taiken*. Tokyo: Sakai Shobō, 1957.

ANDŌ TSUGUO. "*Kaneko Mitsuharu oboegaki*," *Gendaishi no tenkai*. Tokyo: Shinchōsha, 1967.

Itō Sei et al. *Dokkai kōza gendaishi no kanshō.* Tokyo: Meiji Shoin,
    1968.
Hiraoka Toshio. *"Kaneko Mitsuharu," Gendaishi kanshō kōza,* VII.
    Tokyo: Kadokawa Shoten, 1969.
Kitagawa Fuyuhiko. *Gendaishi Kanshō, jō.* Tokyo: Yūseido, 1972.
Nakano Kōji. *"Kaneko Mitsuharu, Rakkasan, Kurage no uta," Kin-
    dai no shi to shijin.* Tokyo: Yūhikaku, 1974.

Index

And hecklers shout, some near my ear,
"No one will be there even if you make it,"
Striking me with the idea that my efforts will be in vain.

(p. 111)